It Will *Never* Happen to Me

It Will
Never
HAPPEN
to Me

Growing Up with Addiction
as Youngsters, Adolescents, Adults

Claudia Black

Third Edition

CENTRAL RECOVERY PRESS

LAS VEGAS

Central Recovery Press (CRP) is committed to publishing exceptional materials addressing addiction treatment, recovery, and behavioral healthcare topics.

For more information, visit www.centralrecoverypress.com.

Publisher: Central Recovery Press
            3321 N. Buffalo Drive
            Las Vegas, NV 89129

25 24 23 22 21 20   1 2 3 4 5

ISBN: 978-1-949481-40-2 (paper)
      978-1-949481-41-9 (e-book)

Library of Congress Control Number: 2020946521

Photo of Claudia Black by Winifred Whitfield. Used with permission.

Every attempt has been made to contact copyright holders. If copyright holders have not been properly acknowledged please contact us. Central Recovery Press will be happy to rectify the omission in future printings of this book.

Publisher's Note
This book contains general information about addiction, addiction recovery, recovery, trauma, parental substance abuse, mental health, familial trauma, and related matters. The information is not medical advice. This book is not an alternative to medical advice from your doctor or other professional healthcare provider.

Our books represent the experiences and opinions of their authors only. Every effort has been made to ensure that events, institutions, and statistics presented in our books as facts are accurate and up-to-date. To protect their privacy, the names places, and institutions in this book may have been changed. Except for the poetry and the story "Best Little Boy in the World" names used in the book are not the true identities of clients. Any identification is from the commonalities of being from an addictive family system. All quotes without names were made by people as young as six years of age.

Cover design and interior by Deb Tremper, Six Penny Graphics.

To Jack, whom I dearly love.

Contents

Author's Note

It will never happen to me are words repeated for decades by those impacted by addiction in the family during their growing-up years. Although it's been four decades since the first publication of this book it continues to be the primer on the impact of addiction in the family.

The earlier preface shares what drove me to write this book, some of my initial insights, what led me to identify and discuss the roles common to survivorship, and what the dysfunctional rules were within the addicted family. At that time, naming these roles and rules was a validation to people's experiences and offered a language in which to talk about those experiences. I believe that is still true today.

It Will Never Happen to Me describes the life of the family member disrupted by addiction and speaks to the ways children attempt to cope, describing their experiences of how they bring safety into their life. Yet those very coping mechanisms, while offering survivorship within the storm, create problems later in life. Willpower and intent don't override their internalized self-defeating beliefs. They don't override the unhealthy modeling children are subject to and don't override the traumatic stress that lingers in their body long after a child has left the family environment.

I wrote this book to help people understand that all children raised with addiction are impacted and to challenge the phenomena of their ability to look good, often from an outsider's view appearing to be doing fine. As young adults, they often have a sense of pride in how well they are doing. They have jobs, go to school, have goals. Yet something else is occurring internally. They chronically doubt themselves, sometimes hate themselves. They have secrets, display forms of self-harm, make decisions based in fear, and are afraid much of the time. They are depressed but surprisingly function in spite of it. In many cases they are simply running as fast as they can—running from any insight or awareness, away from the chaos, the drama, or the void of home. They have chaotic, traumatic family stories but with minimization, denial, and confused loyalty. For most, they don't stop to consider the influence of their growing-up years. Ultimately, many repeat a similar story of their childhood; for others, it's a slight variation. They are living a painful legacy that repeats itself as these children live out their traumas.

As much as children have been negatively impacted, there are many factors that can create resiliency and ameliorate some of the traumatic impact. Children need to be supported in their strengths and protective factors created to override the risks. The impact of family trauma does not need to be a life sentence.

It is possible to live their life differently than to repeat the family script. I want children, young and adult, to live life with open arms, not closed in fear or shame. I believe *It Will Never Happen to Me* will help in that process.

Preface

"I spent my whole life making sure I didn't end up like my dad. And now, the only difference between my dad and me is that my dad died from his alcoholism, and I don't have to die from mine."

It has been many years since I first heard those words. In that time I have listened to similar stories repeated by men and women of all ages, across the world. Regardless of the drug of choice, the majority of kids raised with addiction in the family have said to themselves, *It will never happen to me.* They were going to make sure they did not do what their parents had done. As I sit in family groups, I hear the same story from husbands, wives, and partners. They, too, have been raised in addictive families and have repeated those same words. In their wildest dreams, they didn't imagine it could ever happen to them. But they married an addict—some for a second or third time—even though the words, *It will never happen to me,* were thought and spoken with all sincerity. They are all surprised to see the cycle of addiction repeating itself. It does not take long before their children are also echoing those same words. Another generation of young children continue the fight for esteem amidst chaos and fear.

My work and personal life are guided by the belief that no one deserves to live with fear and shame. I was raised in a family setting where addiction was a way of life. Aside from my father being alcoholic, we lived in a small town where my parents owned a tavern that was central to our logging community. Chronic drinking among adults was common to most and exposure to this was the norm. Unbeknown to my mother, my father's drinking was well established prior to their marriage. He was just twenty-two years of age, she was seventeen. Having been raised with alcoholism and compulsive gambling, the earlier stages of my father's addictive behavior were not concerns for my mother.

It would be growing up with an established legacy and an entrenched addictive family that I would find my way into what was then referred to as the "alcoholism field." I loved my parents dearly as I knew they loved me. Notwithstanding, I experienced a family wreaked with havoc by the emotional, physical, and spiritual ravages of addiction.

When I was originally asked to create a family program in a small chemical dependency (addiction treatment) unit of a hospital, I didn't know to ask questions. I assumed when I was asked to develop family programming that "family" meant children. So I began to invite children into the program to talk about their experiences. My clients in the 1970s were of the age that many had adult-age children who were no longer living in the home. I believed, however, that if they had grown up with ten, fifteen, or twenty years of alcoholism they deserved to have a chance to talk about that experience. Growing up in my family I had learned to be hypervigilant to the expressed and the unexpressed, so I was a good listener. I expected these adult-age children would talk freely, and I would be of some service by listening. They came, but they didn't seem to know what to say. They struggled with their thoughts and feelings. Most would tell me how well they were doing, how they hoped their parent(s) would get better, but that they didn't really have any needs of their own. And, certainly, "it would never happen to them." They wouldn't repeat the pattern of their parents. Most were still caught up in the delusion that they had not been seriously impacted by their parents' addiction.

It was in this context that I first began to use the phrase "adult child." From a practical standpoint, it defined who I was working with—the preteen, the adolescent, or the adult-age child in the family. It also acknowledged and validated that this adult was carrying the pain of his or her childhood vulnerabilities having spent life masking and defending against the effects of a troubled family.

Then there were the teenagers. They were very concerned for others in their family, but in their minds they certainly didn't need to talk about themselves. Or they were angry and had an attitude that said they were doing just fine without me or anybody else.

Lastly, were the younger children, and here is where I found honesty and truth. Before me I witnessed a continuum so blatant and yet so unseen by others it would ignite in me a need to look deeper within and into those with whom I was working. It is from those early experiences the first edition of *It Will Never Happen to Me* was written.

This was a time when saying out loud, "I was raised in an alcoholic home" brought gasps from people. To discuss family problems, let alone to name addiction, was perceived by families as a major act of shame and betrayal.

Since those years, several changes have occurred to make it possible for families affected by addiction to break the cycle of their family history. There are many books on recovery available today compared to the days when not one book could be located. *It Will Never Happen to Me* has two million copies in print. It has been translated into multiple languages ranging from Japanese to Icelandic. Twelve-step groups permeate rural and urban America and are found throughout the world. Mental health specialists, family service agencies, and educational professionals are much more aware of and prepared to address the implications of addiction. Family secrets are much more openly talked about.

Yet, for most children growing up with addiction today, the experiences are extremely similar to the days of the past. They live with fear, loneliness, and confusion. Many continue to witness or experience direct physical or sexual abuse. They fear talking about what is happening and are learning to deny, rationalize, and tolerate the hurtful. Their lives are just as isolated as those of children years ago. As a consequence, the long-range impact for the child has not changed unless there has been some type of direct intervention. Adult children continue to become addicted, marry addicts, become depressed, anxious, and rageful. They often do this as they push to excel and overachieve educationally, professionally, and materially.

As you read, do so to understand, not to feel guilt or blame. This book is meant to offer a foundation for understanding what occurred growing up in an addictive family and to offer hope for recovery. With this in mind know that a person does not make a conscious decision about becoming an addict or a codependent. Without the intrusion of addiction he or she would have made other choices.

It is most likely you will experience a myriad of feelings. I urge you to share your feelings with a trusted friend. I also encourage you to use a highlighter pen to mark the words and messages that speak to you. Having a journal or notebook at hand to jot down your responses to what you are reading and for doing the exercises is invaluable as well.

For too long family members have suffered in silence. Let me close by acknowledging the resiliency in all who grew up with addiction. Regardless of how you have been negatively impacted, each and every one of us has incredible strengths. It is my hope you will draw on those strengths and allow your pride in survivorship to extend beyond the ability to survive and embrace the right to thrive.

I also want to acknowledge each and every one of you who have ever thought, spoken, believed, and hoped *it will never happen to me.* Because of that conviction, and because of your impact on me, together we have the possibility of creating a different journey for ourselves and others.

Introduction

While hundreds of thousands of people are in recovery from substance use disorders, codependency, and adult-child issues, our communities continue to be impacted by addiction. Opiates, cocaine, methamphetamine, and marijuana use is rampant throughout our communities. But, historically, the number one abused drug is alcohol.

In today's phraseology, the word *addict* encompasses both the alcoholic and the person addicted to other drugs or compulsive behaviors. It is recognized that a large majority of people who struggle with addiction to alcohol are actively addicted to at least one other substance. And even if they do not show signs of another form (substance and/or behavior) of addiction, they need to refrain from the use of other substances because those other substances would lead them to relapse in their primary disorder or seek out another drug to become their new anesthetizer. As a consequence, the words *alcoholic* and *addict* will be used interchangeably throughout this book.

When these terms are used within this book they are referring to people who have neither the ability to consistently control their drinking or using nor the capability to predict their behavior once they start. Their drinking/using causes problems in major areas of their lives and yet they continue to do so. This is a person who has developed a psychological dependency on a substance coupled with a physiological addiction. It is someone who has experienced a change in tolerance to alcohol or other drugs and needs to drink or use more to reach the desired effect. Their need to drink or use becomes a greater and greater preoccupation. At one time in their lives they had the ability to choose to drink or use. In time, it became not a matter of choice but a compulsion.

Many people are confused about substance use disorders (SUD) because there is no one specific pattern of behavior. Addicts differ in their styles of drinking or using and the consequences of the addiction vary. Some use daily; others in episodic patterns; some stay dry for long intervals between binges. Some alcoholics drink only beer or only wine; for others, the choice is hard liquor. Still others will drink a wide variety of alcoholic beverages. While addiction appears very early in the lives of some people, for others it takes years to develop. Some claim to have started drinking or using addictively from their first use; many others report they drank or used for years before crossing over the invisible line that separates recreational use from addictive use.

Regardless of the predominant drug being abused or the combination of drugs, it is my hope the reader will see similarities in other substance-abusing families. The commonalities will be in living with extremes, living with the unknown, and with fears. It is living in a system where the addiction has become central to the family and the needs of the individual family members become secondary to the needs of the addict and his or her addiction.

Commonalities

Since the original writing of *It Will Never Happen to Me*, we have become more adept at recognizing multidrug abuse and what is referred to as *process addictions*, and that both substance and process addictions may coexist and are often ritualized. Such addictions could be gambling, gaming, spending, eating disorders, sex, and love and relationships. The commonalities across addictive disorders are:

1. A pattern of out-of-control behavior, meaning that those with addictive disorders are not able to predict their use once they engage in the substance or behavior, nor willingly stop their use.
2. Negative consequences due to the behavior.
3. Inability to stop, despite the consequences.
4. An escalation in indulgence due to change in tolerance, i.e., the need to use or engage more to get the desired effect.

5. Preoccupation—the anticipation of, involvement in, or reflection about their addictive behavior is the focus of their thoughts and feelings.
6. Denial—minimization, rationalization, denial of their behavior as a problem occurs to the point of delusional thinking.

Whether or not the addiction is a substance or process, the behavior of the nonaddicted parent follows similar patterns as well. Spouses and partners of the addict are commonly thought of as codependents. The prefix *co* was originally used to describe a marriage or committed partner in a coupleship who had become increasingly preoccupied with the behavior of the addict and functioned in the role of a primary enabler. Today the term *codependent* has expanded to include the dynamics of giving up a sense of self or experiencing a diminished sense of self. We also recognize that many of the codependent traits are reactions to traumatic stress and are frequently trauma responses.

The partner experience often involves:
1. Loss of sense of self.
2. Being obsessed with another person who facilitates not dealing with own life.
3. Reacting to someone else's behavior instead of acting from personal motives.
4. Being all-consumed with another and putting own priorities on hold.
5. Taking responsibility for other people, tasks, and situations.
6. Engaging in a denial system.

The combination of addiction and codependency often results in neither parent being responsive and available in a healthy manner on a consistent, predictable basis. Children are affected not only by the addicted parent but also by a codependent and the resulting unhealthy family dynamics.

Known Facts about Children of Addiction

The National Association of Children of Addiction has reported seventy-six million Americans, about 43 percent of the United States adult population, have been exposed to alcoholism in the family. There are an estimated 26.8 million people who have or are currently living in a home impacted by substance use disorders. Preliminary research suggests that over eleven million of these children are under the age of eighteen. Compared to children living in families not affected by substance use disorders:

- They are twice as likely to have an alcohol and/or other drug use disorder themselves by young adulthood compared to their peers.
- They are more likely to marry someone who has a substance use disorder.
- They are more likely to enter foster care and remain longer in foster care than do other children.
- They exhibit signs of depression and anxiety more so than other children.
- The rate of total primary healthcare costs for children of alcoholics is **32 percent** greater than children from nonalcoholic families.
- Admission rates to hospitals are **24 percent** greater; hospital stays on average **20 percent** longer.
- In general, they do less well on academic measures.
- They also have a higher rate of school absenteeism and are more likely to leave school prematurely.
- Substance abuse causes or exacerbates seven out of ten cases of child abuse or neglect.
- Children whose parents abuse alcohol and/or other drugs are almost three times more likely to be abused and more than four times likelier to be neglected.

As alarming as that is, the greatest majority of people raised in a family impacted by addiction, in fact, do not experience blatant abuse and don't show blatant mental health issues or become addicted. Yet all have been subjected to traumatic stress throughout the most developmentally vulnerable time in their life. As a consequence, they struggle with self-esteem issues, they have difficulty coping with stress, and their distorted issues around boundaries create havoc in their parenting, friendships, and intimacy skills. Whether the impact is subtle or blatant, there are few adult children who wouldn't benefit from looking at the effect addiction had on their growing-up years. It gives them the opportunity to thrive in all areas of their life, to let go of defenses they learned long ago that unbeknown to them sabotage aspects of their relationships. Regardless of how resilient a child may be and his or her ability to look good to the world, what lies beneath the outer behavior is a delayed emotional and psychological stress response. Children have survived at a very high price to their emotional, social, spiritual and, often, physical well-being.

Whether or not you were raised in an addictive family system, *It Will Never Happen to Me* may offer a framework for people raised in other types of troubled families to better understand their family of origin dynamics. People raised with physical and/or sexual abuse (without addiction), with mental illness—ranging from schizophrenia, anxiety to depression, to raging parents—frequently identify with adult-child issues. People raised with parents affected by chronic health issues or physical challenges, highly rigid and controlling parenting, narcissistic parenting, or those in an enmeshed relationship between parent and child will experience similar dynamics. It is also possible that addiction is in the family but skipped a generation leaving the reader to have been raised by an adult child. The connecting thread between these many different types of families is the experience of chronic loss that fuels emotional isolation, rigidity in thought and behavior, and/or shame—the belief that one is not worthy or lacks value. Whatever the circumstances, coming from a history of chronic loss is like being a first cousin to the person raised with addiction.

As you self reflect and are willing to learn about yourself, you have the opportunity to feel validation never before experienced, to experience clarity lessening the confusion of what has been occurring in present-day life, and to discover a direction and focus that ultimately offers you more meaning.

CHAPTER ONE

Vignettes

"No matter what I do, it is never good enough."

"Something bad is going to happen."

As a boy I remember coming home from school and seeing either the living-room or the dining-room furniture thrown out in the driveway. It would startle me—actually it would blow my mind. My first thought would be to get it back in the house before anyone else would see it, and we (my mom or brothers) would get it back into the house. I would feel slightly relieved. However, for several days, or maybe a week or two, depending on the severity of the act, I would be caught up in the thought of what would happen next, such as would my dad give something of ours away to a stranger? And he did give away things we liked a lot, like a pair of skis, a rifle, and once our dog. He would tell us he hated us, or he would call us worthless so-and-sos. I would always ponder those incidents: Why did he do those things? What did I do? What did we do? What could I do to make him different? I went from a young boy to a young man with my thoughts, alone, socially and mentally. I never got to know myself, and I guess I still don't. I am still a loner. I don't know how to live, to have fun, or to enjoy life.

Will

"I am responsible for other people's behavior."

"There must be something wrong with me."

My father is an addict. He has never admitted to that fact. He and my mom got in lots of fights when I lived at home. The six of us kids were used as pawns in their war games. I always wondered whether or not I was responsible for his using. When the fights were going on, I always retreated to my room. There I felt secure. Now, I am thirty-eight and have been married for twelve years. I have this affliction that whenever the slightest thing happens I always say I am so sorry. I am sorry when the milk is not cold, sorry that the wet towel was left in the gym bag. I just want to take the blame for everything, even things I have no control over.

Kate

"Other people's needs are more important than my own."

"It is not okay to ask for help."

I am a twenty-nine-year-old woman (girl actually) who is the only child of two addicts. When I was little I was lonely and afraid most of the time. But when the rest of your friends seem normal and carefree, and your parents are into their own set of problems, to whom do you tell those things? When I used to be awakened by my parents arguing, I longed to have a sister to talk to. Somehow I always felt if I had a sister to mother, to make things all right, that I would have felt better. I never once thought about someone mothering me or making me feel better. My parents separated when I was in sixth grade, and I continued to live with my father. I was relieved when my mother left because at least then the fighting stopped. But then things kind of got turned around and I found myself being the parent and my father the child. I prided myself on the way I was brought up because I thought it made me strong, independent, and self-reliant. Now that I am older, I am so angry I feel like screaming at someone—but there is no one left to scream at. My father died when I was nineteen. I guess my mother just gave up because she just proceeded to drink herself to death. Well, now I am almost thirty and my drinking has increased; I know it and at the same time I don't want to stop. I enjoy it. It helps me to loosen up and feel better. I started therapy last year. My therapist told me I drink to ease the pain. Maybe that is true. I never even thought about being in pain. The scary part is I seem to be emulating the very behavior and role models I shouldn't. But where do you go to undo this life-patterning style?

Jordan

CHAPTER TWO

Family Roles

We became the late-night regulars at the local hospital's emergency room. For instance, one night Mom dropped a gin bottle on her foot and sliced one of her tendons. Another time she was washing dishes drunk, broke a glass, and sliced a tendon in her arm. Another night she threw a saltshaker at Dad, got him in the forehead, and he needed stitches. Once when I was alone with Mom, she fell through the window and was lying there in blood and broken glass, half on the patio, half in the family room. I phoned Dad and he yelled at me to pull her in from the window so she wouldn't fall farther and slice herself in half. I got down on my hands and knees in the broken glass. I stuck myself through the hole she'd fallen through and moved enough glass away from her so I could pull her inside without cutting her up too badly. Then I cleaned her off and waited for Dad.

Jan

Somebody may ask, "What happened then?" Nothing happens then. Nothing. It is Tuesday night. Or it could be Wednesday or maybe Thursday. But nothing in particular happens. It is just another night in this young girl's life.

But something does happen—children learn to repress their fears, sadness, anger, and humiliation. Yet somewhere in their bodies the depth of those experiences and feelings remains, typically dictating how they will perceive and respond to themselves and others. They walk through life conditioned by years of helplessness and powerlessness. Eighteen-year-old Jan is already abusing alcohol and cocaine, is bulimic, sexually promiscuous and, ultimately, suicidal.

While the following experience may not be as extreme, Matt would also experience the consequences of living in an addictive family.

> *I didn't know Dad was addicted to drugs or alcohol until my parents separated. My mom kept it a secret, and my dad just didn't come home much. He was a doctor and I thought all doctors worked a lot. When he was home I was to stay out of his way, not to be a problem. I learned never to question and never to expect anything. I was just supposed to accept his absence and disregard for us. Mom vacillated between depression, being super mother, and having a short temper. I could see her stress, but it was never discussed. I really thought I was not affected, but then I began to have problems in my relationships. I always seemed to need one but didn't know how to be close. I became anxious about everything and then that would end the relationship and sabotage my performance at school. I began to experience depression and still struggle with it today. I realize I missed out on a whole lot of basics, such as feeling I was worthy or that my needs were of value or that I could talk about any of it.*

The short vignettes in many ways summarize life for a child growing up with addiction. The unpredictability, the confusion, the false guilt, the sense of defeat, the chronic fear, and loneliness that is pervasive in their childhood now permeates their adult life. Then the legacy begins to repeat itself.

Adult children don't have a sense of what normal is; they don't know what a healthy family would be like. Healing can begin by understanding the differences between healthier functioning families and those that are less functional.

Functional	Dysfunctional
The system is open, expanding, and changing.	The system is rigid, closed, and secretive.
Feelings are allowed and shared.	The system controls which feelings are allowed.
Mistakes are acknowledged, possibly disciplined, and forgiven.	Mistakes are punished, judged, and shamed.
The system serves/exists for the individual.	The individual serves/exists for the system.
Individual boundaries are supported.	Individual boundaries are not respected nor valued.
Each generation redefines.	Intergenerational repeats.
Family roles are chosen by the individual.	Family roles are assumed via the function of the system.

The healthy functioning of a family is sabotaged when addiction permeates that system.

Reacting to the Troubled Family System

Consistency is one of the clearest indicators of a smoothly functioning family. In contrast, inconsistency and unpredictability best describe living in a family impacted by addiction. As the problems surrounding the addiction cause more and more inconsistency and unpredictability in the home, the behavior of the nonaddicted family members typically becomes an attempt to restabilize the family system. Members of this family act and react in a manner that makes life easier and less painful. What children do while living in an addictive environment they do because at that time it makes sense.

In most well-functioning families, emotions are expressed clearly, with each person being given the opportunity to share his or her feelings. Emotions are accepted by an attentive group that offers understanding and support. Family members can freely ask for attention and in return give attention to others.

In a home beset with addiction, feelings can get big very fast or literally disappear into nowhere. Emotions are repressed and become twisted. They are often not shared and, unfortunately, when they are expressed, it is done in a judgmental manner with blame being placed on one another. Apprehension exists around even the most minor of situations or decisions, where that which doesn't matter gets a lot of attention and that which does gets swept under the rug and ignored.

> *Everyone was worrying about someone else's feelings and discounting their own. My mother would feel sad and worry about something going on with me. Rather than see it as my mother's sadness and worry, my father wanted me to be different so she wouldn't feel sad or worry. No one wanted to take responsibility for their own problems—they always blamed someone else.*

> *You don't have anything to be crying about. Get out of here before I slap your face.*

> *You don't have anything to be angry about, after all your father does for you. You should be ashamed. You want me to tell him what you just said?*

While constructive alliances are part of the healthy family, members of an addicted family system often lack alliances or alliances will be unhealthy. Family members frequently operate with marked independence from each other, very separated, as if they are on two different planets. Or they are highly enmeshed, not allowing anyone to have their own sense of autonomy. Invariably you will find alliances where family members join each other and together those two (or more) unite against another. A son becomes the surrogate spouse to his mother and together they bond against the father/husband. Siblings may turn to each other for support but may also compete for attention that is limited. They may manipulate the parents to get what they need, jockeying for an edge over another sibling.

Families have rules, which need to be fair and flexible. These rules also need to be verbalized. Rules such as "No hitting" or "Everyone will have a chance to be heard" lead to healthier functioning within a system. In addictive family structures, rules are usually fueled by shame, guilt, or fear. Rather than a verbalized rule that says, "There will be no hitting," there is an unspoken, silent rule that says, "You won't tell others how you got that bruise." The rules often reinforce secrecy. "What happens here stays here; you tell no one." "Only my voice is important in this family. I make the rules, you obey them." "It's not okay to question authority."

Many times there are clearly defined roles within the family. It is typical for adults in the family to divide or share the roles of being breadwinner and administrator—the one who makes the decisions within the home. Children raised in homes where open communication is practiced and consistency of lifestyle is the norm usually have the ability to adopt a variety of roles, dependent upon the situation. These children learn how to be responsible, to organize, develop realistic goals, play, laugh, and enjoy themselves. They learn a sense of flexibility and spontaneity. They are usually taught how to be sensitive to the feelings of others and are willing to be helpful. These children learn a sense of autonomy and independence and, at the same time, how to belong to a group. Children growing up in addictive homes, however, seldom learn the combinations of roles that mold healthy personalities. Instead, they become locked into roles based on their perception of what they need to do to survive and bring stability to their lives.

Those who work with young people in schools, in the juvenile justice system, and family service agencies often report contact with a high percentage of children from addicted homes. But when they speak of this young person they are more apt to describe him or her as an angry, acting-out child, showing behavioral problems. I contend most children impacted by addiction in the family are *not* seen by school counselors, are *not* addressed in juvenile justice systems and family service agencies. In the school setting, if they are seen it is often because they are asked to be of help to the teacher or the administrator. Their leadership skills are tapped to be of assistance. The majority are not children who become runaways or perform poorly in school. They are not blatantly angry. They do not exhibit problematic behavior. They do not draw enough attention to themselves to be identified as being in need of attention. As a result, they are a neglected population. If they are busy and look good or are simply less visible, they will be ignored.

Feeling trapped in a highly confusing system, family members do what is needed to be safe. They do what they need to preserve the family system. This typically means they hide their feelings behind an artificial behavior pattern.

Family Roles

The majority of children tend to adopt one or a combination of the following roles: the *responsible child, adjuster, placater, or mascot.* These are roles that allow children to draw either positive attention or no attention to themselves. A smaller percentage finds ways to draw negative attention by adopting a fifth role, the *acting-out child.* Some children clearly fit into one of these roles. For most, though, there is a primary and then secondary role. Someone may identify strongly with being in the responsible child role, but in certain instances quickly move into being an adjuster. It is very common to see the responsible child also be a placater. There are occasions in which a child switches roles. This means that for a period of time in his or her life he or she was responsible then moved into the acting-out role. Every role has strengths, but equally every role has deficits or vulnerabilities. Fitting with the research about birth order, an only or oldest child is most likely to be a very *responsible child.* This child not only assumes a great deal of responsibility for himself but does so for other family members as well. This is the nine-year-old going on thirty-five, the twelve-year-old going on forty. From the onset of addiction in the family, this child has been an adult. It is the seven-year-old putting Mom to bed, the nine-year-old getting dinner ready every night, the twelve-year-old driving his father around because Dad's too drunk to drive himself. Overall, this is the child whose adult-like behavior is compensating for a parent's immaturity. This role is one in which the child seldom misbehaves but, rather, takes on many of the household and parenting responsibilities for the other siblings and, very possibly, for the parents.

Next is the child who is usually not the oldest or the only child. This is the child who does not develop the need to be responsible for himself or others. The need is not as great because there is often an older sibling providing the needed structure in the environment. This middle or younger child finds the best role to play is that of the *adjuster* or often thought of as the *lost child*. It is easier to simply follow directions, handle whatever has to be handled, and adjust to the circumstances of the day. She spends a lot of time alone, in her room on the computer, or off in the corner reading. Simply out of sight. This coping pattern allows the child to appear more flexible, more spontaneous, and possibly, more selfish than others in the home.

A third common pattern within this increasingly chaotic home life is that of the *placater*. This is the family comforter, or otherwise known as the household social worker. It is this child who, with great sensitivity to the feelings of others, takes responsibility for other people's painful feelings, doing whatever he or she can to lessen their pain. The placater is a good listener, taking away his mother's sadness, brother's fear, sister's embarrassment, and his father's anger. A fourth role is that of the family *mascot*, often thought of as the comic in the family. The mascot is great at distracting others from the family pain with his or her humorous antics. In doing so, this child distracts himself from his pain and confusion as well.

We can easily find value in all of these role characteristics and typically don't see them as destructive. In fact, labeling children with words such as "responsible," "caring," "able to adjust to crisis" and "funny" allows them, as adults, to pat themselves on the back for having been such good "survivors." The survival mechanisms of those who "look good" often though lead to unhealthy extremes. The need for this coping behavior frequently results in emotional and psychological deficits. It is the understanding of such deficits that allows one to understand how survivors end up living out a family script. It is this family script that draws them into behaving addictively themselves, marrying someone who is or becomes an addict or having emotional and psychological problems in their adult years.

While those who ascribe to looking-good roles are reacting to the turmoil in their lives in a way that doesn't draw negative attention to them or their family members, a small number of children will find ways to say loudly that something is very wrong. Metaphorically and literally, they walk through their growing-up years and, often, adult years, with their fists clenched and raised, with a finger protruding, saying, "There is something very wrong in my life and you are going to notice me." Instead of behaving in a manner that actually brings greater stability into their lives, or at least one that does not add to the turmoil, acting-out children often display highly problematic behavior. Their behavior more adequately typifies the true state of the family.

As you read further, do not be locked into the labels of these roles. There are many possible adjectives that may have more meaning for you. Common terms may be "hero (responsible)," "scapegoat (acting-out)," "wallflower (adjuster)," "peacemaker (placater)," "clown (mascot)," "comic," "scorekeeper," "chameleon," etc. What is most crucial is to ascertain if you identify with any particular role (named by me or you) as a part of responding to an addictive family and, to ultimately, recognize both its strengths and vulnerabilities.

Responsible Child

Everything must be in order in my household or it brings great anxiety to me. My growing-up years were nothing but total CHAOS.

Children need consistency and structure. As a person's addiction progresses and the partner becomes more and more preoccupied with the addict, children experience decreasing consistency and structure in the family unit. This makes their lives less and less predictable. Some days when Dad is drinking or using, no disruption or tension occurs. On other days, he becomes loud, opinionated, and demanding in his expectations of the children. Mom, at times, reacts to this disruptive behavior by being passive and ignoring it, while other times she makes arrangements for the children to go to the neighbor's home until Dad goes to bed or leaves, or she tells them to go outside and play. The children don't know what to expect from either parent when Dad drinks.

When the parents do not provide structure and consistency, children will find ways to provide it for themselves. The oldest child or an only child, very often becomes the *responsible* one in the family. This child takes responsibility for the environmental structure in the home and provides consistency for others. When Dad starts raging while drinking or after being away for a few days and comes home in withdrawal, this youngster gathers the coats and pajamas of the other children and leads them to the neighbor's house. While Mom and Dad are out getting loaded together, the responsible child directs the other children to their bedrooms, ensures they complete their homework, instructs them to change into their nightclothes, and go to bed. This is the nine-year-old girl who has a flow-chart across her bedroom wall marking what she needs to do on a daily basis to take care of the house. She assumes a lot of responsibility because she feels the need for structure. In this situation, she perceives that her mother, who works more than eight hours a day, is always sad and tired. Mom never complains, but this young girl knows it helps when the carpet is vacuumed, the dirty clothes ready for the laundry, the shopping completed, the dishes washed. She also knows everything seems better when her brothers and sisters receive direction from her about what they can and cannot do. When this nine-year-old takes charge, her siblings feel safer and they are less apt to bother their mom and dad. Overall, everyone in the family seems a lot happier.

Sometimes the responsible children are directed to assume this role; other times, they assume the role voluntarily. Maddie, age thirty, said, "My mom took me out of a foster home I had been in for three years just so I could be home to take care of my two younger brothers." Another adult-child told me, "My being such a good housekeeper, cook, and parent to my sister made it easier for Dad to be out of the house when Mom was loaded. He didn't know what to do, so he just worked later and later and had more and more business trips." It is typical for the parents to take great pride in their adult-like youngsters. Responsible children make life easier for the parents by providing more time for the addicted and nonaddicted parent to be focused on themselves and each other.

Whether responsible children are blatantly directed into this role or more subtly fall into it, it is a role that brings them comfort. Playing the responsible role provides stability in the life of the child and in the lives of other family members. Responsible children find comfort in their organizational skills. They practice this role so consistently that they become exceptionally adept at planning and manipulating. In order to provide the structure they seek, they often manipulate their brothers and sisters. This ability to organize, to affect others, and to accomplish goals provides these children with leadership qualities—qualities that get them elected as class leaders, captains of teams, and presidents of clubs.

Responsible youngsters become adept at setting tangible goals: "I'll be sure I get the grocery list done tonight and do the shopping tomorrow after school," and "I'll be sure the boys get their baths tonight, and the girls tomorrow night." These goals are realistic and attainable. In an addictive home, one is most realistic if one thinks of goals on a short-range basis. "What can I get done today?" "What will I get done tomorrow?" If these children begin thinking about what they want to accomplish in terms of the next few weeks or months, they know their home situation may not remain stable enough for them to follow through with their plans. Too many long-range plans are negatively affected by addiction. "I don't remember my mom or dad ever planning a birthday celebration for me. I certainly didn't expect one. But a couple of times I called my mom on my birthday and asked her if I could bring home a couple friends from school, as if it would be a party. I knew her answer always depended on Dad's mood, and she could only predict it a few hours ahead."

In setting short-term goals that are realistic the child has a better chance for success and experiences a sense of accomplishment. Responsibility, organization, setting, and achieving goals are attributes encouraged and rewarded in our culture. Again, this is not the behavior where a child is identified as a child in need. Being goal-oriented allows a child diversion from the family pain; it provides him or her with psychological relief; he or she gets positive feedback. Most importantly, at this stressful time, it makes life easier and responsible children find meaning in their behavior.

Responsible children have learned to rely completely on themselves. It is what makes the most sense to them. They have learned the best way to achieve stability is to provide it for themselves: "If you want to get something done, do it yourself." They cannot consistently rely on their mother or father. The parents may respond to the children emotionally and psychologically at times, but the unpredictability and inconsistency of the parents' behavior are destructive elements.

Children also come to believe that other adults will not be available to them when help is needed. If they cannot trust the people in their lives who are supposed to care about them, how can they trust that others will be there for them? They assume others won't see what they see, believe what they experience. When others do not intervene, they interpret that to mean others don't care about them.

Most adults perceive responsible children as very mature, dependable, and serious. Peers often view these children as not quite so much fun as their other friends but recognize them to be smart. The responsible child socially either becomes active in structured social activities or does not have a significant social life. This child needs to be in organized situations where he or she feels in control and a sense of safety. He also finds himself to be a leader in these organized fun events reinforcing his role.

Adjuster

Put me in any situation now and I can adjust. But please, don't ask me to be responsible for it or change it.

When others in the home—typically an older sibling or the mother or father— provide structure, younger children may find it is not necessary to be responsible for themselves or their environment. The child called the *adjuster* finds it much easier to exist in this increasingly chaotic family situation by simply adjusting to whatever happens. This youngster does not attempt to prevent or alleviate any situation. The child doesn't think about the situation or experience any emotions as a result of it. Whatever happens, when it happens, is simply handled. The adjuster's bottom-line thinking is "I can't do anything about it anyway," which in many cases is realistic. A clinician would describe the adjuster as the child who seems most detached from the family. The other children in the home may perceive this child as more selfish, while the parents don't seem to notice this child as much.

While the responsible child, placater, mascot and, certainly, the acting-out child are quite visible, the adjusting child is seen less often. This is the youngster who most likely goes to his room unannounced, who spends less time at home and more time outside the house with his friends. This is the family member who seems oblivious to the conflicts and emotions at home. "What fight? Oh yeah that . . . Oh well."

As the child heads out the door to stay at a friend's house for the night and the father hollers, "Where do you think you're going? Who gave you permission to go anywhere? You aren't going anywhere. You are staying right here tonight!" the adjuster simply comes back, returns his clothes to the closet, and quietly calls his friend to give some excuse for not coming over. He knows that Dad had told him earlier in the day that it was okay to spend the night at his friend's house. He knows that Mom is also aware of that. Yet, he also knows it won't do any good to argue with his dad now that he has been drinking. This same child, when his dad hasn't shown up for one single ball game all season, simply tells Mom it was no big deal and not to feel bad because he doesn't feel bad. "Besides, if Dad had shown up, he probably would have been drunk anyway." It's just easier to accept the situation.

Children describe the many times Mom becomes angry with Dad because of his being loaded so she packs the children and their belongings into the car and races off to a relative's. The next day, she packs them up again and returns home because somehow Mom and Dad got things worked out. Clothes are back in the drawers, and they're all sitting at the dinner table—everyone acting as if the previous night didn't happen. I have heard so many times, "It doesn't help to question it. It is just easier that way. And it certainly doesn't help to interfere." Adjusting children find it wiser to follow the flow of what is happening and to make sure they don't draw attention to themselves. This child is just as often thought of as the *lost child*. This behavior is less painful for these children and makes life easier for the rest of the family as well. The role of the adjuster is permeated with denial but without the focus on others.

Acting without thinking or feeling is typical of the true adjuster. A young woman once told me about the time she and her father had gone to a ball game together, thirty miles from home. She said her father dropped her off at the game, and he went to a bar. He was intoxicated when he picked her up after the game. She said this didn't cause her any concern. In fact, it was typical. But on that night, as they headed for home, he stopped at another bar, fifteen miles away. He gave her the keys to the car and said, "Now, I want you to drive home and tell your mom I am at the D.B. Bar and Tavern and I'll be home in a little while." The young girl got in the car and drove home. Even though she didn't know how to drive, she didn't question her father or his instructions. She said, "He had left the car running and it was an automatic. I just got in and pointed it toward home. I ran in and out of ditches and drove mostly on the shoulder, but I got home. I was crying the whole way home, but when I got there I calmed myself down, went into the house, put the keys on the counter, walked into my mother's bedroom, and told Mom that Dad was at the D.B. Bar and Tavern and would be home in a while. I then went to my room and went to bed." She said her father and mother both knew she didn't drive: her father ignored the fact; her mother didn't even ask how she got home. She said, "Once I got in the house, I didn't think about what had happened."

"Put me in any situation and I will handle it. I won't feel, get upset, or question it; I will just respond to it." The adjuster does not think of saying, "Dad, I can't drive home. I don't know how to drive." She doesn't want to upset her father. She doesn't think of simply waiting for him to come out of the bar after it closes. After all, she was given instructions and she has learned the best way to keep peace in the family is to respond to those instructions without question. She doesn't think of calling her mother and asking for advice on how to handle the situation—she does not want to cause her mother any problems. It is just so much safer to handle the situation alone.

At school, the adjusting child is as nondescript as he or she is at home. Regardless of intelligence, this child is academically about average, not demonstrating brilliance or ignorance, consequently not drawing any negative or positive attention through schoolwork. As a result, this child does not greatly impact or impress teachers.

In social situations at school, the adjuster associates with other children but remains somewhat detached, more aloof, and in the outer parameters of social circles. Adjusters don't lead and are most frequently followers.

Placater

> I am really good at distracting people when they are afraid or angry. I can sit for hours with someone when they are alone. People like me. I am nice. Kind. Sensitive to others. A good listener. Wonder what I would be or feel if I wasn't so nice and responsive to others. Maybe no one would like me.

In every family there is usually at least one child who is particularly more emotionally sensitive than the others. The *placater* finds the best way to cope in this inconsistent and tension-filled home is by acting in a way that will lessen his own tension and pain and that of the other family members. Not able to build a wall to protect his feelings as well as those who take on the other roles do, this child will spend his early years trying to fix the sadness, fears, angers, and problems of brothers, sisters and, certainly, of the parents. It is an all-consuming role that not only allows him to feel better about himself, but he is appreciated by those he is attending to. In this process, the family system seems more stable and, in the moment, more safe.

While Mom and Dad are arguing, and the other children are afraid of what will happen, the placater does what he or she can to diminish the fear. When a sibling is embarrassed by Mom's drunken behavior at the supermarket, this most-sensitive child acts to make the situation less painful for the sister. A brother is angry because Dad broke another promise, so the placater reacts to help dispel the brother's anger. This pattern develops at a surprisingly young age, as demonstrated when five-year-old Michael told his crying mom, "Don't worry Mom, I won't remember all of this when I grow up." The placater is always there to make life easier for others by doing whatever is necessary to take the emotional pain out of the home.

As this child grows to adulthood, others experience him as a nice person. After all, he spends his time trying to please others, trying to make others feel better, and usually he succeeds in doing just that. The placater becomes exceptionally skilled at listening and demonstrating empathy and is well liked for these attributes. If this child is a full-fledged placater, he will never disagree. In fact, he is the first to apologize if he feels an apology is needed, especially if it will protect another person. Eleven-year-old Tom apologized to his mother on the average of ten to fifteen times a day. "I'm sorry you broke the milk bottle," "I'm sorry you don't feel well," "I'm sorry I am thirty seconds late to the breakfast table," "I am just plain sorry." Tom's mom was an addict, and Tom said, "I just couldn't figure out why she was always loaded and knew there must be something I did to make her so unhappy. So I just tried to make it better by apologizing."

Parents are often proud of the placater for being so selfless, caring so much about others over himself. They never have to worry about the placater being disappointed because he doesn't appear to get upset when plans fall through and doesn't let anyone know he is bothered by anything. Dad doesn't take the children to the game as promised; the placating youngster squelches his own disappointment and focuses on his younger brother for the rest of the day. When Mom says, "No," unjustifiably, this sensitive child may have tears well up in his eyes but goes to his room to cry alone. He isn't going to argue or run to the other parent. In every way, he seems to be a very warm, caring, nonproblematic child.

By the time I was five I had learned how to take care of others. My parents repeatedly told me the story of what happened when I was in the hospital at age five for a tonsillectomy. While waiting in the pre-op room, another five-year-old girl began to cry in anticipation of her surgery. I went to her and very expertly calmed and soothed her fear. In retrospect, I only did what I'd been trained for. That's what I did at home with my mother. I had to mask all of my own feelings in order to bring happiness to everyone else.

These characteristics of sensitivity are displayed outside the home just as they are within the walls of the family. In fact, these are the qualities that make the placating children so well liked by others. Being a placater is certainly safe. If he allowed himself to risk self-disclosure, he would have to experience the pain of that reality. Placaters are highly skilled at diverting attention from themselves and focusing it onto others. Imagine the resultant personality when this role is combined with that of the responsible child—the combination of the child responsible for the tangible environment and for the emotional needs of others, he becomes the household social worker. It is easy to understand why placaters are well-liked at school and at home; it is even easier to recognize why they don't draw attention to themselves as a child in need.

Mascot

I didn't pay any attention to what was really happening at home. I was busy running from the moment by finding something that made people laugh. When they felt better I felt better. It was clear to me that someone needed to distract the rest of them from the absurdity.

Cute, funny, quick-witted are the words family members use to describe the child who takes on the role of *mascot* in the family. Other words for the mascot are the family clown or comic. Siblings often think of this child as the family pet. In his or her humorous style, this method of distraction prevents both the mascot and other family members from focusing on the pain. Mascots usually received a lot of reinforcement from others to continue in this role because it provides relief. Humor and wit lead to positive attention; this is extremely important to a child who is not getting the attention deserved.

Deb could get anyone to laugh. She was adept at knowing who needed her in the moment; she was intuitive in her ability to find those who were hurting, angry, and lost. Everyone liked her. As she moved into her teenage years, she was always the life of a party. When she was around, no one was focused on anything but her. While placaters do what they can to take care of family pain by being caring, sensitive, and good listeners, the mascot takes care of the pain by making faces, telling jokes, or teasing in a humorous way that gives other people the sense they are liked. This behavior is not used to belittle or hurt anyone. This is a vibrant child with energy and whose actions certainly do not say, "Look at me, I am in pain," but rather says, "Look at me, aren't I cute. How can you not like me?" For the mascot, it is possibly the only time he or she has felt noticed, offering him or her a sense of belonging. Mascots aren't succumbing to the seriousness of their life; they are using what both they and their family needs and that is distraction from the real issues—the pain of addiction.

Distractibility is their second name. They often show a lot of energy in their role and are always prepared to not just distract others from what could be occurring but need to be distracted themselves.

The mascot role is a great mask for the entire family. As others meet this young person, they see charisma, wit, and brightness. They see adaptability. Other people are often attracted to someone like this. Should they know this child is living in a family impacted by addiction, they are quick to believe this child is just fine because, after all, this child seems happy.

Acting-Out Child

Alcohol was uncool because that is what our parents used. So my friends and I started taking drugs. They could wipe out any feelings. I could decide what to feel. I felt relaxed, not so manic or intense. I took meth in dosages even heroin addicts were afraid of and that made me feel powerful. People saw me as crazy but that was okay. I felt strong. Friends called me Loadie, and I wanted to wear that name as a star on my lapel. I looked up to my friends— they were fun, cool, and I wanted to be like them and liked by them. So I was off and running and never looking back.

The *acting-out* child is the stereotype of a child from a troubled family. She feels her anger and she is going to let the world know about it. These children either don't have the words to describe their life, or they don't trust anyone will listen let alone be of any help. So they act out by lying, cheating, defying authority and rules. They engage in behavior that is outright abusive and disrespectful of others and others' property. Their behavior assists the family in staying in denial about the central issue of addiction, as it provides distractions from the real issues. If there is a blatantly angry child in the family, it is often easier for parents to focus on that child and the ensuing problems created rather than worry about the father's or mother's drinking or using. Such children are the ones who perform poorly or drop out of school or experience teenage pregnancy. Many become a part of the criminal justice or psychiatric systems. While acting-out children are the ones most likely to be addressed and receive help from one or more professionals, the addiction within the family is typically ignored.

Unacceptable behavior is learned and parents are the primary role models in this learning process. Parents usually set the mold, either through action or inaction. Parental immaturity—often expressed in extreme selfishness, lack of consistency, cruel teasing, inappropriate discipline, lack of structure, or lack of healthy limit-setting—is frequently characteristic of life in addictive homes. Most children in trouble have an extremely poor self-image, reflecting their parents' feelings of inadequacy. Acting-out children find it nearly impossible to communicate their feelings to adults in a healthy way. While other children with the same problems learn how to repress problem areas and focus on other areas of their lives, acting-out children use unacceptable forms of behavior to say, "Care about me" or "I can't cope." These children are attempting to be the voice for the family, saying, "Help! Look at us!" Often they have less denial than others about what is occurring in the family. They can be exceptionally creative and even show leadership ability. They simply tend to lead in the wrong direction.

Where other children tend to draw positive attention to themselves or escape attention altogether, the acting-out child contributes to the severity of his own situation by eliciting the kind of attention that causes parents to cry, nag, belittle, or even strike their child. This ultimately undermines the child's developing self-esteem.

The opinions and acceptance of one's peers are extremely important to most young people. While the acting-out child pushes many of his peers away, ultimately, in a desire for belonging, he will gravitate toward others who have equally low self-esteem. In this process, he not only garners a sense of belonging but also an identity.

Unfortunately, most of these acting-out children don't get help. For those who do, the help they get is only for their problematic behavior, not for being part of an addictive family system, which is the basis for their behavior.

Over the years, people have frequently challenged whether or not these roles are different in other families. As stated previously, there are defined roles within any family as a result of parental expectations and the influence of birth order. The difference is that in the addictive family system the roles are fueled and created from a basis of fear and shame. As a result, children become locked into these roles based on their perception of what is necessary for survivorship. Consequently, they rigidly adhere to the strength of a role to such an extreme that what was positive often becomes a strong negative behavior.

The value of addressing roles is to recognize their strengths, vulnerabilities, how they are integral to the family system, what you want to keep and, ultimately, what you need to learn to compensate for the vulnerability of the role.

The bottom-line: *All children impacted by addiction in their growing-up years are affected.*

CHAPTER THREE

Family Rules

Don't Talk, Don't Trust, Don't Feel

The Best Little Boy in the World (He Won't Tell)

Peter M. Nardi

Michael was doing very well in school. In fact, he was the brightest kid in class, the teacher's favorite, one of the best behaved. He never created any disciplinary problems and always hung out with the good crowd. The best little boy in the world. "Why can't we all be like Michael and sit quietly?" Sister Gertrude would say in her most melodious voice. Conform, be docile, do well, and be quiet. Hold it in. Don't tell a soul.

And now he was waiting at the school corner for his mother to pick him up. This was always the hardest moment. What will she look like, how will she sound? Michael could tell right away if she had been drinking. The muffled voice, the pale, unmade-up face. He really didn't know what it was all about. He just knew that when Dad came home he would fight with her. Argue, yell, scream, and run. Michael could hear them through the closed doors and over the humming of the air conditioner. He wondered if the neighbors could hear, too. Hold it in. Don't tell anyone.

He was still waiting at the corner. She was fifteen minutes late. It was so good to go to school and get out of the house. But when three o'clock came he would feel the tension begin to gather inside him. He never knew what to expect. When she was not drinking, she would be smiling, even pretty. When drunk, she'd be cold, withdrawn, tired, unloving, and not caring. Michael would cook dinner and straighten up the house. He would search for the alcohol, like egg-hunting on Easter morning, under the stuffed chair in the bedroom, in the laundry bag concealed among the towels, behind her hats in the closet. When he found it, he'd pour it down the sink drain. Maybe then no one would know that she'd been drinking. Maybe no one would fight. Don't tell a soul.

She still hadn't come to pick him up yet. She'd never been thirty minutes late. Sometimes she'd sleep late in the morning after Dad had already left for work, and Michael would make breakfast for his little sister and himself. Then a friend's mother would take them to school. The biggest problem was during vacation time, especially around the holidays. He wanted to play with his friends. But he was afraid to bring them home. He was afraid to go out and play, too, because then she would drink. Michael didn't want to be blamed for that. So he stayed in and did his homework and read. He didn't tell his friends. Hold it in.

And still he was waiting alone on the corner. Forty-five minutes late. Michael decided to walk the ten blocks home. He felt that he was old enough now. After all, he took care of his little sister a lot. He took care of his mother a lot. He was responsible. He always did what people told him to do. Everyone could count on him for help. Everyone did. And he never complained. Never fought, never argued, never yelled. The best little boy in the world. Hold it in.

When he got nearer to home Michael's heart felt as if it were going to explode. Her car was there. The house was locked tight. He rang the bell. He rang and rang as he felt his stomach turn inside out. He climbed through a window. No one seemed to be home. He looked around the house, in all the right hiding places. Finally, in the closet in his own bedroom, he saw his mom in her slip, with a belt around her neck and attached to the wooden rod. She was just sitting there, sobbing. She had been drinking. But maybe no one would find out. Michael wouldn't tell anyone, ever. Hold it in.

Family Rules

Thousands of children like Michael are being, or have been, raised in homes where at least one parent is addicted to substances or a behavior. And like Michael, these children appear to suffer no apparent ill effects. They are typical in that, like most children, they leave home in their latter teenage years. When they do venture out on their own, they face the task of making decisions about school, work, careers, lifestyles, friends, and where and with whom they are going to live. Along with thousands of other young people, they are also making decisions about relationships, possible commitments, and whether or not to have children. In young adulthood, they are beginning to make some of the most important decisions of their lives and then spend years implementing those choices. At this stage of life they are focusing on external events, not sitting back and reflecting on their growing-up years. If they recognize that they grew up with addiction, they breathe a sigh of relief and pat themselves on the back for their survivorship. They then continue going on about their life, yet frequently remain socially and emotionally entangled with their family.

About the time a young person reaches his or her mid-twenties, the negative effects of growing up in an addictive home start to become apparent. These now-adult children begin to experience a sense of loneliness that doesn't make sense to them. They become aware of feelings that separate them from others. There is a low depression occurring more frequently and lasting longer. They experience self-loathing and despair but are gifted in not letting others see it. Feelings of fear and anxiousness occur more frequently, but they don't know why they are having these feelings. They often feel empty and have difficulty maintaining close relationships.

In fact, many describe themselves as relationship nomads, going from one relationship to another, yet never feeling close or emotionally intimate. They also find they are in relationships with others who are hurtful, disrespectful, abusive, as well as engaging in addictive behaviors. A lack of meaningfulness begins to permeate every aspect of their lives. For many, the repetition of the addiction has begun. Their drinking and using has become an important part of their life, or they are engaging in other behaviors in an addictive manner, such as work, spending, and gambling, or they have disordered relationships with food. Should any of this be occurring, their rationalizing and defending is blocking the ability to see this as a problem.

To break this cycle it is necessary to recognize the many processes that have occurred.

Don't Talk

The Family Law: DON'T TALK ABOUT THE REAL ISSUES.

The real issues: Mom is drinking again. Dad didn't come home last night. My mom showed up loaded at the school event. My dad was drunk at the ball game and passed out in front of my friends.

Some say it is a rule; I believe, for most addictive families, it has become law. As one nine-year-old daughter said, "When you have a rule in your house for so long, to not talk about Dad's drinking, it's r-e-a-l-l-y hard to talk now—even when he is sober."

In the earlier stages of addiction, when a parent's drinking or using seems to become a more noticeable problem, family members usually attempt to rationalize the behavior. They begin to invent excuses: "Well, your dad has been working hard these past few months," or "Your mom has been lonely since her best friend moved away." Rationalizations become the normal way of life. Family members may see the problems but do not connect them to the addictive behavior. There are many excuses offered but, occasionally, one seems even more absurd than the others. Alexa told me that when she was about ten years old, her mother told her that she believed her father's irrational behavior was because he had a brain tumor and was going to die. The mother told the children their father wanted them to hate him before he died so it would be easier for them to accept his death when it happened. Alexa said, "It didn't feel right, but who was I to question my mom? She had enough problems as it was. And, besides, she had this odd smile when she told me, and I seldom saw my mom smile. I didn't want to be the one to take that smile away." Alexa said she simply thought her father was likely dying from a brain tumor. She now understands that while her father acted crazy, his erratic behavior was due to his drinking. His increasingly controlling and tyrannical moods, his inconsistent behavior related to his blackouts, as well as his hallucinations (which were withdrawal-related), added to his appearance of craziness.

It is often easier to invent reasons for crazy behavior rather than naming it as addiction. Should the drinking or using take place outside of the home and the parent doesn't act falling-down drunk or in a stupor or if the kids don't see the parent, children may more readily accept what the other parent tells them—drinking/using is *not* the problem.

Children are like adults in that they, too, will believe addicts are the stereotypical homeless person or street junkie without a job or family. If children do not understand addiction, it is difficult for them to identify their parent as addicted.

Mara said she knew her father wasn't an alcoholic because "My Dad loved me and I knew that." No one ever explained to her that alcoholic people are also capable of loving others. She believed because her father loved her he could not be alcoholic. Mara had heard about alcoholism only once at church where a recovering alcoholic told his story. But what she heard was that particular person's story of his drinking. She could not relate that story to her father. Her father certainly didn't sound, look, or behave like that man. Such fragmented information is typical of children's lack of knowledge concerning addiction.

Another way family members rationalize the erratic behavior is not to discuss or in any manner talk about what's really happening at home. Thirteen-year-old Steven said, "I thought I was going crazy. I thought I was the only one in my house who knew Dad was an alcoholic. I didn't think my mother or two sisters knew." I asked him why he believed this to be true. He answered, "Because no one ever said anything." Steven described an incident that occurred when he and his father were at home alone. In a semiconscious state from drunkenness, his father had fallen, hit his head on the coffee table, thrown up, and was on the floor bleeding. Steven's mother and sisters had returned home within moments after his dad had hit his head. Seeing him on the floor in his own vomit, bleeding from the back of the head, they ran over, picked him up, cleaned him up, and carried him off to the bedroom. What was most significant though is that no one said anything about it then or later. No one spoke to anyone else. No one said, "Oh my gosh, Steven, what happened? Are you okay? When did this happen?" Nothing was said. After I was told of this by Steven, I asked the other family members if they remembered this incident and they all did. Then I asked why they had not talked about this incident with Steven. They all responded, "Because he hadn't said anything, and we hoped he hadn't noticed."

"If I get honest about this, it is also a setup for then being honest about the other things I don't want to be honest about," Steven's mother ultimately confessed. "It only makes me feel more guilty and more hopeless." Helplessness, despair, and hopelessness cause family members to believe if you just ignore it, it may not hurt; if you just ignore it, it may just go away.

Fear and control often fuel the Don't Talk rule. Skip described his father as controlling the family with silence. "My dad didn't talk to me at all, and my mother wouldn't acknowledge that there was anything wrong. My life was filled with this engulfing terribleness, and I thought it was me. I wanted my father to tell me there was something wrong. I wanted him to tell me it was his fault. I wanted to hear it was not my fault. Later, as I got older, I needed him to tell me he was proud of me. I didn't get any of those things. I only got his silent rage." Skip's answer to this was to keep a lid on his feelings. Keeping the lid on fueled a major eating disorder. By fifth grade, Skip weighed 250 pounds, and he would ultimately weigh 400 pounds. It was only when his father died that Skip would begin to shed his weight. With the need for emotional control over, the behavioral manifestation of his powerlessness no longer gripped Skip and his recovery would begin.

Many adult children have told me that they were instructed not to talk about things that would upset their mother or father; or they simply learned by themselves that things went much easier when they did nothing to rock the boat. Andrew said, "Dinner was pretty quiet. Anything we said rocked the boat. And then, if we were too quiet, that rocked the boat!" These children not only don't talk about boat-rocking issues, but they don't talk about or share their fears, worries, or hurts with anyone.

In many families, the rule of silence is a quiet collusion. Children will share the same bedroom with a sibling for years, both hearing the arguing taking place between their parents. Or, they hear their mother crying night after night. But they only hear. They never speak to one another about it, although they may each cry—silently and alone. In one family, the six children were between the ages of twelve and twenty-one when the father sought treatment for his addiction. Three to four months prior to seeking help, the father would return home late at night after having been drinking for several hours. Not having seen his children all day, he'd make his nightly rounds, passing from one room to another. He would scream, shout, and harass each child before moving on to the next room. All of the children were awake as he went from room to room, but they never spoke to each other about these nightly episodes. The family simply acted as though nothing out of the ordinary was happening. Well-adjusted children who experience childhood problems would, most likely, talk about these things with other family members. In another family, young Billy told me how he was taking the air out of the car tires so Dad wouldn't drive when he was drinking. His youngest sister, Ann, was putting water in Dad's vodka bottle; his oldest sister, Lisa, was hiding her father's drinking stash. Each was unaware of the other's actions concerning their father's drinking because they were unable to talk about the real issue—his substance abuse.

Because of the denial, seldom are any of these children's problems recognized. Moreover, the family problem—addiction—is never discussed. These children do not perceive others, inside or outside of the family, to be available to them for help. Many adult children have questioned where their aunts and uncles were when they needed them. Many wondered why grandparents weren't more concerned for them. Nora told me no one would have believed what her home life was like. "They wouldn't believe me, because if it was so bad, I couldn't be looking so good. They never saw my mother getting drunk every day; they never saw her raving like a maniac, passed out upstairs. They never saw her bottles all over the house. They just never saw."

While many children fear not being believed, they may also feel guilty. They believe they are betraying their parents and their family if they talk honestly. Children feel very loyal to their parents and, invariably, end up defending them, rationalizing that it isn't really all that bad, and continuing in what has now become a denial process. Finding the family situation so confusing, they feel inadequate in attempting to verbalize the problems—they just don't know how to tell others. This makes it very easy to succumb to a sense of hopelessness or helplessness.

As the alcoholism in my family progressed, the family got more and more silent and the house got more and more quiet. We withdrew from each other. It got to the point that we didn't talk to each other about much of anything. We couldn't even talk about safe things, such as a television program. How could we ever talk about the things we knew weren't safe?

It is as if you are wearing a pair of eyeglasses with clouded lenses from which to view the world. Perceptions are altered, reality distorted. You continue to discount and minimize; learning to tolerate inappropriate behavior. You learn to live in denial. It is most despairing to be a child in an addictive family, to feel totally alone, and to believe talking to someone will not help.

Sometimes I pretend my mom is not drinking when she really is. I never even talk about it.

Don't Trust

I am always on my guard with people. I want to trust them, but it is so much easier to just rely on myself. I'm never sure what other people want.

Children raised in addictive families learn that it is not safe to trust others with the real issues in their lives. To trust another means investing confidence, reliance, and faith in that person. Confidence, reliance, and faithfulness are virtues often missing in the addictive home. Children need to be able to depend on parents to meet their physical and emotional needs in order to develop trust. Parents are not consistently available to their children because they are under the influence of alcohol or other drugs, physically absent, mentally and emotionally consumed with their addiction, or preoccupied with the addicted person.

When Jayne comes home from school, she can't count on her mom to be attentive about what she has to say. Her mom doesn't smile after hearing about something funny nor is she sensitive to Jayne's sadness. Her mom is preoccupied with what happened or didn't happen last night as the result of her dad's drinking.

Karl doesn't trust people to see his feelings as important. He may be angry about something that happened on the way home from school, but he usually doesn't say anything about it because "There's enough to be angry about at home. Who needs more? Besides, they wouldn't understand."

Sean cannot trust the decisions his parents make. He can't rely on his dad to remember a promise to go to a ball game on the weekend or the permission he gave Sean to spend a night at a friend's house. Nor can he count on his mom to support him if his dad goes back on his word.

Sara cannot rely on her mom to be sober for her birthday, Thanksgiving, or Christmas. While Sara cannot rely on her mom for sobriety during special occasions, Jason knows his mother will be loaded on those holidays. He said the uncertainty, the never knowing for sure how his stepfather was going to handle his mother was most confusing for him.

Nate, age thirty-two, described an incident when he was eleven years old. He had returned home from school and found his mother intoxicated. As he came through the door, she started an argument with him. She began to scream and shout at him, and he began to scream and shout back. This was a typical after-school scene, but this time his mother picked up a broom and began hitting him about the head and shoulders. While his mom was screaming and hitting, Nate was ducking and hollering back. He ran for the phone and called his father. (His parents were divorced.) Nate was surprised when his father answered, but he did at least answer! Imagine the scene of this eleven-year-old yelling into the phone explaining what was happening, ducking the broom, while his mom is screaming and continuing to hit him. His father shouts back, "Don't worry, she won't remember it tomorrow."

Twenty-one years later, when Nate related this incident to me, he spoke with no expression or affect in his voice. I asked, "Nate, does that sound like a healthy or appropriate response to you?" He looked at me quizzically and slowly said, " I don't know. I guess I have never really thought about it." Of course he had not thought about it. Nate could not rely on his mother to respond appropriately to him emotionally, psychologically, physically, or to meet his needs in any way when he was an eleven-year-old boy. He could not rely on his father to understand his needs either, let alone offer protection while he was being physically abused. It wasn't emotionally safe to allow himself to respond with hurt, anger, or disgust to his mother's beating or his father's lack of concern. But he did find it safe to detach and not to think about the incident. Like so many others with similar experiences, Nate learned to not trust.

In order for children to trust they must feel safe. They need to be able to depend on their parents for help, concern, and guidance in response to their physical and emotional needs. In families affected by addiction, children often cannot rely on parents.

Kristin tells how she never feels safe bringing friends home because "It is always possible Mom will be drunk and do something to embarrass me." Scott said, "It is never safe to play in our yard because Dad always seems to be sure to belittle me when my friends are around." These children live in a chronically fearful environment. For some, their lack of safety is more psychological; for others, it is psychological and physical. Children often tell of frightening times with a parent who is driving recklessly or when fires are caused due to drunken neglect. Children's physical safety is directly threatened when verbal harassment turns violent, when furniture is being broken or, certainly, when persons in the home are physically and/or sexually assaulted.

It is difficult to trust a person who constantly embarrasses, humiliates, disappoints, or puts you in physical jeopardy. It is even more difficult to trust when family members minimize, rationalize, and/or blatantly deny certain events are taking place.

Part of feeling safe is feeling secure. Security is seldom present for any length of time in addictive homes. Tim comes home from school one day to discover his dad has lost his job for the fourth time in three years. It means the family will be moving again. For Tim, it means giving up some newfound friends at a school that was just beginning to become familiar to him. And it means giving up the opportunity to make more friends through Little League, which he just joined—another disappointment. Tammy finds out her dad gave away her purebred pet rabbits to a drinking buddy. She had been raising them from kits (baby bunnies) with the intention of entering them in the county fair—another hope shattered. David learns the family's long-planned summer vacation has to be canceled because Dad loaned the vacation money to a stranger he met at a local bar—another promise broken. Children are continually confronted with reasons to be insecure in their surroundings, to not trust.

Joe described his inability to trust this way. "Trust? My dad couldn't ever seem to take care of himself wherever he was. There was always a problem—at home, at work, with the car, with grandparents, with friends. If he couldn't take care of himself, how was he going to take care of me? No, I couldn't trust him for anything. And my mom, she was there, but that's all I can say. She was physically there, but I don't remember her ever trying to help us cope or understand. She was simply there."

Children constantly hear mixed messages, which teach distrust. A parent often gives a child false information intentionally in a feeble effort to protect the child from reality. A mother may tell the children she is happy when she is actually miserable. A father may reassure a child that nothing is wrong when the child can see Mom is acting strangely. The child is confused because one message is coming from his parent's words and a contradictory message from the body movement and tone of voice. Such confusing messages propel the child into a life of second-guessing what is really happening.

The single, most important ingredient in a nurturing relationship is honesty. No child can trust, or be expected to trust, unless those around him are also open and honest about their own feelings. Addicted people lose their ability to be honest as the disease progresses. As the addict continues to drink or use, he has to rationalize his negative action and do it extremely well in order to continue his behavior. An addict's life is consumed with feelings of guilt, shame, anxiety, and remorse, causing him to drink or use more in an attempt to escape. It becomes a never-ending cycle because of the psychological and physical addiction. Enabling parents are fearful of being honest with their children. They don't want them to experience the same pain they are feeling. Moreover, they don't want to acknowledge that the problem exists in the first place.

While children don't require verbalization of all the feelings their parents experience, they do need validation and/or clarification of certain specific situations and feelings. This validation or clarification doesn't happen in a home where *talking* and *trusting* do not exist.

A person takes a risk when he reaches out to trust another. Those persons who have learned to take the risk have experienced trusting to be a good process. They have also experienced a sense of security and a feeling of self-worth, both derived from feeling loved. All young people need to feel valued, to feel they are precious and special. While parents may tell them they are special and loved, it is the parents' behavior that allows a child to believe it.

Children need focused attention, as it represents not only physically being with a child, but also interacting with the child in a way that says, "You have all of my attention—mentally and emotionally." It says to a child, "I care. It's important for me to be with you." Children are highly sensitive to the degree of focused attention they receive. A child receives no sense of value from parents who are forever absorbed in their own affairs. While children don't need exclusive attention, it is the lack of focused attention that causes them to feel unimportant. As a parent's addiction progresses, it fuels isolation that makes them less available to their children. The other parent's increasing preoccupation with both the addict and their own helplessness and hopelessness decreases their availability for the children.

Although these children are not totally ignored, as the addiction progresses, the availability of focused time decreases. When these families do spend time together, that time is often centered on the addictive behavior. Tim, age fifteen, told how he was spending special time with his father. Both liked to fish and did so quite often during the summer. Although Tim always looked forward to the two of them spending time alone together, he was almost always disappointed because his father normally brought along a drinking buddy. Dad and his buddy got so involved in their drinking and carrying on that Tim might as well have been totally alone. Tim spent time with his dad, but the time spent did not allow Tim that special time meant just for him and his father. The father's attention was always focused elsewhere—with or without Tim around.

Children need focused attention most when they are under stress. Unfortunately, in an addictive family this is when they are least apt to receive it. Stress often becomes the norm in this environment and the attention centers around the addict. Thus, instead of turning attention to the child who may be having a problem, attention is turned away from the child with no opportunity for support, nurturing, or problem-solving.

Due to broken promises and unpredictability, children are confused. They find they don't trust caring acts and are suspicious of focused attention when it occurs. A child may enjoy a day at the zoo but will question the motivation behind the trip. Although both parents may have agreed on the excursion, the child perceives only the addict's sense of guilt or the other parent's dominance over the situation. Or, the child thinks the parents do care in this one instance, but that thought is overshadowed by the knowledge that neither parent may be relied on to be available at another time. They may wonder, *Did Dad bring me this present because he didn't come to my piano recital last night or because he saw it and wanted me to have it out of his love for me?*

While children can and do demonstrate a multitude of strengths, they will nonetheless struggle in some areas of their lives because their circumstances have made it impossible for them to feel safe, secure, or to rely and be able to trust. Trust is one of those vital character-building blocks children need in order to develop into healthy adults. Being raised in an addictive family structure often denies or distorts this portion of a child's development.

I have a hard time trusting my mom.

Don't Feel

No, I wasn't embarrassed. I was scared for my father, but I wasn't scared for myself. It didn't dawn on me to be scared for me. I wasn't disappointed. I didn't really think about it. I never got angry with him. There was nothing to get angry about. I didn't cry much. What was there to cry about?

It has been my experience that by the time a child raised in an addictive family is nine years of age, he or she has a well-developed denial system about his or her feelings. Should the child identify having feelings, those feelings are often taking on the feelings of others. As nine-year-old Chris said, "One time my dad got upset when he was drinking and he slapped me. I looked at my mom and she started crying. So I cried. I wasn't crying for me, I was crying for my mom."

Denying feelings is a way to bring stability and consistency into children's lives. It also makes it easier to cope; it's a survival mechanism. The role adoption described earlier assists children in coping with the inconsistencies in their lives. Learning to focus on the environment or on other people or learning to detach from the family assists children in not feeling.

The family law Don't Talk and the premise Don't Trust teach children that it isn't safe to share feelings. Children learn not to share and, inevitably, deny their feelings. They don't think family members, other relatives, or friends will validate their feelings. They don't believe their feelings will receive the necessary nurturing. Children don't perceive others as resources; therefore, they live their lives emotionally isolated. Being alone with feelings of fear, worry, embarrassment, guilt, anger, loneliness, etc., leads to a state of desperation or being overwhelmed. Such a state of being does not lend itself to survival, so children learn other ways to cope. Some learn how to discount and repress feelings, while others learn simply to not feel. These children do have access to their feelings but only with the help of a trusted person. For the majority of children growing up with addiction, however, trust and trusted persons are not a consistent part of their lives.

Demi is a cheerleader for her high school's basketball team. One evening, at an out-of-town game, her father arrives noticeably drunk. After having spent much of the evening yelling out to Demi during her routines, her father, who by this time is unable to walk himself out of the gym, drapes himself over the top of Demi, relying on her to get him out of the gymnasium and to the car. As she is slowly moving the two of them out of the gymnasium, he begins to yell and jeer at several students just behind them. His remarks are crude and vulgar and then he begins to scream racial slurs. With determination, Demi pushes her way through the crowd, holding her father tight to her. Behind her she hears the escalating remarks of the crowd. Suddenly, they are outside. She rushes him to a car driven by one of his friends, leaves him, and then quietly makes her way to the school pep bus.

Embarrassment, humiliation, fear, and anger are the common emotions of a child in this situation. But for Demi, none of these emotions are conducive to helping know how to handle the problem. Instead, the reaction of this most-responsible eldest child is to take care of the situation and to get her father out of the gymnasium before he or others gets hurt.

Demi has learned if she lets feelings take over when an incident like the one just described occurs, it will only result in pain for herself. It doesn't occur to her to talk to anyone (a chaperone on the trip, a school friend) about the incident because she believes no one would really understand or, worse yet, that they would make unkind judgments about her father.

Only a few tears fell that night as she headed home. None of her schoolmates mentioned the incident and she most certainly didn't tell her mother about it. She knew that to discuss the incident would only bring more pain to the family. Demi has found it's a lot safer to ignore her feelings. For her, the feelings are too confusing, too complicated, and very scary. She hasn't found anyone she can trust to share those scared feelings.

Any young person would feel disappointed if his parent didn't show up for at least one school event in the entire school year. A child from a healthy family would not only be disappointed but angry as well. But for the child of an addictive family, this is just another one of those events to try not to feel bad about. It is easier not to feel anything than to dwell on the pain or the unfairness of it. And if the child does feel, it is easier to be angry with the nonaddicted parent when he or she misses an activity or to take the anger out on a classmate.

It would be normal for Jerry to be disappointed, afraid, and angry when, as a child, he has been sent to stay with a relative because Mom's drinking became worse. When he returns in a couple of weeks, he's told his mother won't be drinking. But Jerry finds his mother exactly the way she was when he left home—drunk. The six-year-old in this situation might tell Dad he is angry (he hasn't yet learned to deny), but Jerry at age nine would just ignore it. He simply no longer allows himself to respond emotionally.

In these incidents of denial, children are building up walls of self-protection. They are learning unhealthy coping mechanisms to protect themselves from the fear of their reality. The reality is that their parents are failing them. As the addiction progresses, the substance or the behavior becomes the parents' obsession. When family members experience the results of this obsession, they ask the questions, "Why?" "Why does my mom disappoint me at important times?" "Why does my dad embarrass me like that?" "Doesn't he love me?" "Why is my dad drinking so much?" "Are my parents ever going to get better?" "Is she crazy?" "Is it my fault?" "Am I crazy?" It is frightening for family members to ask such questions of themselves. It can be even more frightening to allow themselves to honestly answer.

There is so much to feel about, to be emotional about.

Afraid

- When Mom and Dad fight.
- To ask Mom when Dad will be coming home only to find out he may not be coming home.

- To tell Mom, "No" about anything, for fear she'll get loaded and leave.
- Of being in the car with Mom when she is driving while impaired.
- Of getting hit when Dad is drunk and violent.

Sad

- Because we don't have any money; Dad can never keep a job.
- When I see my mother crying.
- When I have to sit in the car for hours and hours when Dad is in the bar.
- Because my dad would rather be away than at home.

Angry

- At Dad, for making excuses for my mom when she is just drunk.
- At others, for calling my mom a junkie.
- At Dad, for making promises and always breaking them.
- At Dad, for always being so critical.
- At Mom for using again after she stopped.

Embarrassed

- When Mom attended the school open house intoxicated.
- Because Dad has passed out in the front yard.
- Because Mom looks so sloppy and half-dressed.
- When my dad tries to act sober, but he isn't.

Guilty

- Thinking if I hadn't talked back to my mother this morning, she might not have left and got in that car accident.
- For never being able to do enough to please my dad.
- For hating someone I am supposed to love—my mom.
- For being ashamed of my parents.
- For being alive.

These are only a few of the multitude of feelings family members may experience on a daily basis—yet learn not to express. As a result, they learn to discount and inevitably deny those feelings entirely. The reason for denying is to convince themselves, as well as others, that their unhappy family life can be made happy by pretending or denying reality. People tend to deny and minimize both situations and feelings in order to hide their own pain. They don't want to be uncomfortable. The greatest problem here is that when someone minimizes and discounts feelings for not just weeks, but months and years of their life, it becomes a skill they take with them into adulthood that will permeate every significant area of their life.

John, why do you think other people feel angry, scared, and disappointed, but you don't?
  Maybe because I have to be tough!

Don't Talk, Don't Trust, and Don't Feel are the three major rules in the troubled family system. Yet other rules are also often experienced.

Don't Think

Many children learn that it is not okay to think about what is happening. When it is not safe to talk or feel, it simply becomes easier not to think about what they are witnessing or experiencing.

Jessica told me, "We were taught not to think, not to speak, and not to feel. There were all of these kids in the same house, and it was as if there was this conspiracy among us. We were each other's witnesses, but it was as if our eyes and ears were closed. That was our form of self-protection. We silently accepted our doom. My mother, who was our role model, was a quiet, religious woman. She was physically present when the abuse was going on, but she never spoke of it and somehow shut her ears to it."

Don't Question

The rules Don't Think and Don't Question go hand in hand. When Mom doesn't come home, don't question; when Dad contradicts himself mid-sentence, don't question; when plans are canceled, don't question. It's just easier that way. "Don't ask for anything if you can get away with it without asking. If they said the family was going somewhere and then didn't, you had to accept it. If they said pick a bag of weeds for no good reason, you went and picked the bag of weeds. If they hit you, you did nothing, and you felt nothing." Life is easier, safer to not question. Children learn to tolerate the inappropriate, the hurtful. In time, they become numb.

Don't Ask

Don't Ask means more than don't ask questions. Don't ask for more information—you may be ridiculed or shamed. Don't ask for something you want or need—you know you will be denied. Children either learn not to ask or, as in Jason's case, nearly have an anxiety attack when doing so.

Jason, who is eleven, needs twenty dollars to play in the band at school for a special event. He waits for his parents to come home. He knows they will be loaded; there is never a good time to ask for anything. He has rehearsed his request for hours. He has several times talked himself out of the need for the money to play in the band. He literally finds himself shaking as his parents enter the house. As they come through the door, his father sees him and quickly yells, "What are you still doing up at midnight, Punk? You ought to be in bed." Jason responds, "I've got to talk to you. I need some money for a pair of black pants so I can march with the band." Dad responds, "A marching band? Does that school think we're a money tree? Tell your teacher to come over here and tell me to my face that I've got to foot the bill for some pansy band uniform. I'll tell him a thing or two." Jason's mom yells at her husband to shut up, and the focus shifts, both parents now arguing with each other, forgetting about Jason and his request. After a few experiences such as that, you not only learn not to ask, you learn not to expect. Jason is not angry or even disappointed with his parents. He is angry with himself for being hopeful.

Don't Play

Many children learn it is not safe to play. "Who will take care of my little sister if I am outside playing?" "I can't take time to play. I need to stay with the adults to know what is going to happen next." For some, it is too painful to go play with others when their thoughts and feelings are focused on what is happening at home. It is easier to just stay at home— watch and be vigilant. Others find that their only validation comes when they are being mature, with the implication that to play was immature and irresponsible.

They are not supported and cherished for being who they are, only acknowledged and validated for being a premature adult.

Don't Make a Mistake

Many children learn mistakes will not be tolerated. Derrick, age thirty-four, can remember his first mistake. "I was six. It was my first and my last mistake. I was eating a bowl of cereal with my dad and I spilled the milk. He backhanded me. I flew off the stool, hit my head up against the refrigerator door, and had a headache for the next three days. I have never made another mistake." This is a setup for learning to not initiate.

The dysfunctional family rules are a way of life in addictive families. You learn how to live without the truth being told. You learn to keep your mouth shut and pretend problems do not exist. Denial of what is going on in the home creates a severe distortion of perception. You learn to not see the world clearly. As you move into adulthood, you find yourself wearing a distorted pair of glasses with which to view the world. You continue to discount, minimize, and tolerate inappropriate behavior by not questioning. As part of this process, you develop a painful, high tolerance for inappropriate behavior. When the three basic rules, Don't Talk, Don't Trust, Don't Feel, are combined with the other dysfunctional rules, it is easy to see how a child easily becomes dispirited and moves into a coping role.

CHAPTER FOUR

Progression of the Roles

Children raised in addictive homes enter adulthood coping with life's problems in ways that have proved to be of great value to them. These include being responsible, adjusting, or placating, being a mascot, as well as not talking, not feeling, and not trusting. Reaching young adulthood, adult children go on about their lives continuing to applaud themselves for being survivors. As adults they find no reason to change these patterns that have always ensured survival.

Responsible Child

The oldest or only child, the one who became the little adult, continues into the grown-up world carrying a lot of responsibility. The ability to be responsible has been a great strength in that this young adult has already demonstrated maturity in handling many different kinds of situations. He or she continues to take charge and often assumes leadership roles. As a child, this person learned to set realistic goals during very early years. As a young adult, he or she has realized a number of accomplishments far sooner than most people. But, there also has been an evolution. This adult person now becomes tense, experiences increased anxiety, and often feels separated from others by an invisible wall.

During their growing-up years, children who adopted the responsible role were so busy being adults that there was no time to be children. They didn't have time to relax as children and, as a consequence, they don't know how to relax as adults. These children have been taking life so seriously for so many years that now, in adulthood, they are awkward and uncomfortable and have a very difficult time joining in fun.

I still try to take a lot of responsibility for people and things. I am only beginning to learn how to play. I find it difficult to enjoy hobbies or fun activities with any great consistency.

Chris, who had so organized and structured her own childhood, became very rigid, lacking in flexibility. As a child, she needed to be in charge or at least feel she was in control. If not, she had a sense that her entire world was collapsing. As an adult, this phenomenon continues. Chris finds herself needing to take charge, to feel in absolute control. If not, there is a pervasive sense of losing control and being totally overwhelmed. For this adult child everything is all or nothing, one way or the other, there is no in-between.

The idea of loss of control is intolerable to me. I get panicky when I even think of it.

Max finds his need to be in control puts him in a one-up position, which leaves others in the one-down. Being one-up is thinking of one's self as better than another; the person in the one-down role thinks of self as having less value than another. There is no room in Max's life to be in a relationship where the partners are equally valued. That would ultimately mean giving up control, which, for Max, would be giving up survival. One-up, one-down, and win-lose relationships are common in many professional, social, and intimate relationships. Remember, those responsible youngsters have become rigid, serious, goal-attaining young adults who have confidence in their ability to accomplish a great deal by being in charge. No sense of equal partnership exists for this person.

Another masterful and admired skill is that this adult child is often verbally articulate. Yet, the ability to speak well often means talking around the truth rather than owning the truth.

Jenna is an only child of an alcoholic father. At the age of thirty-one, she had become a lawyer in private practice, an apparent success. Unfortunately, she was alone in that private practice because two attempts at working with other colleagues had failed. She lacked close female friends, and her third marriage was failing. Jenna had developed those traits similar to so many other children raised with addiction. She had not learned to trust others so she simply tried to control them in an attempt to get her needs met.

As with many children of addiction, she also found it easier to rely on herself, not involving others. Jenna is outwardly successful, yet inwardly, someone who cannot bring herself to trust that others will be there for her. She can't depend on others and therefore has no recourse but to relate on an unequal basis. She doesn't know how to have fun, nor can she talk about the real issues for herself, and she certainly can't talk about her feelings. In her personal and professional relationships, she is almost forced to associate with others who are equally emotionally inaccessible. Should she find an, articulate, emotionally open, caring, fun-loving person in her life she would feel awkward and not know how to respond.

A sharing, intimate relationship would be too uncomfortable so the responsible child removes him- or herself from that relationship. Responsible children often align themselves with people who are accepting of their rigidity, seriousness, and emotional detachment. If not, they then find themselves alone. It is easy to see why so many responsible adult children find themselves depressed, lonely, anxious, tense, and fearful. It is also easy to see how and why they often enter into unhealthy personal relationships.

The following table notes the strengths and vulnerabilities common to the Responsible role. Vulnerabilities pertain to emotional and psychological skills not learned due to the rigidity of the role.

Strengths	Vulnerabilities
• Organized	• Inability to listen
• Leadership skills	• Inability to follow
• Decision maker	• Inability to play
• Initiator	• Inability to relax
• Perfectionist	• Inflexibility
• Goal-oriented	• Need to be right
• Self-discipline	• Severe need to be in control
	• Extreme fear of mistakes
	• Lack of spontaneity

Beliefs That Drive Behavior

If I don't do this, no one will.

*If I don't do this, something bad will
happen or things will get worse.*

Response to Feelings

I must stay in control of my feelings.

*I was the all-American kid. In high school, I maintained a 3.6 grade
point average and was a star on the championship baseball team.
I was always trying to please my parents. Dad was a cocaine
addict and a compulsive gambler. Mom worked seven days a week
to support the family. After high school, I went into business for
myself, but something was wrong. I was empty inside and didn't
know why. Whatever I did just wasn't good enough. The more
I achieved, the worse I felt. The accomplishments didn't mean
anything. I couldn't fill the emptiness—it was always there. Finally,
I couldn't face life anymore and turned to using pills to numb out.*

Adjuster

Children who found it much easier to shrug their shoulders and withdraw upstairs to the bedroom or slip out to a friend's house usually continue these survival patterns into their grown-up years. Adult adjusters find it easier to avoid situations where they need to take control. They function better if they take whatever occurs in stride. They have become adept at adjusting, being flexible, and spontaneous. They find pride in these traits. As Jason said, "I went to nine different schools as a kid. I never knew how long I would stay or where I was going next. It wasn't bad. I learned how to make friends quickly. I met a lot of interesting people." Now, as an adult, Jason still finds it necessary to keep moving. "I get bored in one spot. I get bored if I am at a job more than nine months; I get bored with the same woman after nine months. I am even getting bored with this city. I have been here two years now."

MOM AND DAD PLAY TUG OF WAR WITH ME. I LOVE THEM BOTH AND WANT THEM TO BE GOOD TO EACH OTHER. I FEEL GUILTY AND SAD A LOT CAUSE I DON'T KNOW WHAT TO DO SO THINGS WILL GET BETTER AND ALL OF US CAN BE HAPPY.

MY BROTHER WON'T PLAY TUG OF WAR. I DON'T WANT TO BUT I CAN'T GET AWAY.

VICTORIA, AGE 16

Children who adopt the adjusting pattern find they have neither the opportunity to develop trust on an ongoing basis nor the ability to develop healthy relationships.

Jeff, who was raised in an abusing, alcoholic family, said, "More than anything, I was scared. I didn't have lots of friends, but I didn't want lots of friends. I did have two friends growing up. I think they came from homes like mine. I don't know really—we never talked. We hung around the playgrounds a lot. When I had to be home, I watched television if I could. If someone wanted to change the station, I let them. I just tried to be quiet. I liked to draw a lot so I did that. I never showed my drawings to anyone. They would have made fun of me."

Adjusters, who as children, never knew how long they would be living in one place, or how long their mother would be sober, or how long their father would be staying away, learned how to handle (or adjust to) whatever situation they were currently in.

> I usually had a movie playing in my head. I was always the star, the heroine—strong and powerful and beautiful. I also had an imaginary friend who provided constant companionship and comfort. Fantasizing was my only protection from living continually in pain.

Adjusters often have neither a sense of direction, nor a sense of taking responsibility for the direction they would like to take their lives. They feel no sense of choice or power over their own lives. While the more-responsible children have developed a sense of being able to affect the events in their lives, adjusters usually do not have a sense of any control.

Life is a perpetual roller coaster for the adjuster. Not because they like living that way, but because they feel they have no other options. They perceive themselves as having no alternatives. They never learned that choices were available to them. So now, as adults, they don't talk about real issues in their lives, and they certainly do not seriously examine their own feelings. Adjusters find themselves associating with others who are as emotionally closed as they are. This limited association is the only type of relationship they find safe.

Due to being such followers, they also need someone else to lead. That can be a responsible adult child, or it could be the acting-out adult child who despite their acting out still takes charge. With an acting-out partner, the state of living in constant agitation becomes their comfort zone because they are perpetuating childhood roles of adapting to inconsistent people. They know how to handle chaotic situations—adjust. This kind of self-negating adjusting leads to depression, isolation, and loneliness.

The following table notes the strengths and vulnerabilities common to the Adjuster role. Vulnerabilities pertain to emotional and psychological skills not learned due to the rigidity of the role.

Strengths	Vulnerabilities
• Flexibility	• Inability to initiate
• Ability to follow	• Fear of making decisions
• Easy-going attitude	• Lack of direction
• Not upset by negative situations	• Inability to perceive options
	• Follows without questioning

Beliefs That Drive Behavior

If I don't get emotionally involved, I won't get hurt.

I can't make a difference anyway, why try?

It is best not to draw attention to myself.

Response to Feelings

Why should I feel? It's better if I don't.

Placater

The child who was busy taking care of everyone else's emotional needs—
the warm, sensitive, caring, listening child, the one everyone liked—grows
up continuing to take care of others, either personally or occupationally.
As a very special friend of mine once said, "Those of us in the helping
professions did not gravitate here accidentally. There must have been
something wrong with us to be so preoccupied day in and day out with
the pain of others." Though this statement was said in half jest, it carries
an enormous amount of truth. For the child who was particularly adept
at making others feel comfortable, it's only natural to gravitate toward
situations that would enable him or her to continue in that manner.

*There is something about me that seems to attract sick individuals
or simply people with some type of problem.*

Forty-four-year-old Eve was raised in a home by two parents who
were addicted. When one takes care of others over the years, it is not
unusual to arrive at the point Eve eventually reached. She proceeded to
enter into three marriages with three different practicing alcoholics. When
her third husband was hospitalized for his addiction, I asked her during
a private session, "While your husband is in this program, what can you
do for you so you'll feel better?" Eve looked away. She began to grimace.
She didn't answer my question, nor did she look at me. So I repeated the
question. "Eve, while your husband is in the hospital for the next three
weeks, what can you do for you so you'll feel better?" Again she looked
away, but this time in addition to making grimacing gestures with her face,
her shoulders began to twitch and jerk. The jerking was almost spasmodic.

Reaching out to steady her, I said, "Eve, you don't have to take care of
your husband anymore! You don't have to take care of him. We are going to
take care of him. And you don't have to take care of your two boys tonight.
You've already told me they are with friends. It is seven o'clock now. Between
seven o'clock and ten o'clock tonight, what are you going to do for you so
you will feel better?" There was a pause but no grimacing, no jerking. Eve
simply said the only thing she could have said. With tears running down her
cheeks, she whispered, "I don't know, I don't know. When in my forty-four
years can I ask myself what it is that I want? When I do, I feel so guilty. "

Of course she didn't know. All her life, the question of what she could do for herself was not a question she could safely explore. Adults who grew up in the role of placaters typically go through years of adulthood never seriously considering what they want. Instead, they discount their needs and focus on the needs of others. They have trained themselves only to be concerned with providing for others, consequently never getting what they want from life. For the placater, survival was taking away the fears, sadness, and guilts of others. Survival was giving of one's time, energy, and empathy to others. Surviving had nothing to do with their personal needs. And as Diane, a forty-eight-year-old woman married to a recovering addict said, "I am that compulsive giver. I need to become more selfish. I must quit serving everyone else at my own expense, but I don't know how." Giving to others is not bad but giving at the expense of our own well-being is destructive. It is relatively easy to understand why these children develop depression as adults. Although they appear to be living their lives the way they want, they still feel apart from others; they feel lonely. They don't have equal relationships with others. They always give too much and refrain from putting themselves in a position to receive. In personal relationships, placaters seek out people who are takers and who often refuse to take emotional responsibility for themselves. They are most comfortable being with others who are accepting of this one-way relationship.

The following table notes the strengths and vulnerabilities common to the Placater role. Vulnerabilities pertain to emotional and psychological skills not learned due to the rigidity of the role.

Strengths	Vulnerabilities
• Caring	• Inability to receive
• Empathetic	• Inability to focus on self
• Good listener	• Guilty
• Sensitive to others	• Strong fear of anger
• Gives well	• High tolerance for
• Warm	inappropriate behavior
• Nice smile	

Beliefs That Drive Behavior

If I am nice, people will like me.

If I focus on someone else, the focus won't
be on me and that is good.

If I take care of you, you won't leave me or reject me.

Response to Feelings

I must take care of others' feelings.

She Was My Mother Bless Her Soul

I sometimes sit in the corner in the dark
and recall my mother
with a brown bottle in her hand
or the sounds of clanking ice at 2 a.m.
She'd call me baby if she wanted another beer or a slut if she
hadn't had enough.
She'd make me cookies on Christmas before she'd get too drunk.
Many nights
she would fall asleep on the floor.
I'd cover her with a blanket
and put a pillow under her head.
I'd awaken in the morning to the sounds of her screaming.
She wasn't an easy woman to please.
Most of the time we didn't get along.
Sometimes I miss her and the loneliness.

Jane

Mascot

By adulthood, the child who everyone in the family usually thinks of with a smile on their face, the one they are grateful for the humor he brought to the dark times, finds himself lost. The responsibilities of adulthood become a challenge as this role doesn't afford the adult child specific skills. He seeks out environments where his distractibility via wit and humor is valued; however, that becomes lacking unless his peer group remains young.

The following table notes the strengths and vulnerabilities common to the Mascot role. Vulnerabilities pertain to emotional and psychological skills not learned due to the rigidity of the role.

Strengths	Vulnerabilities
• Perceptive	• Distracting
• Sense of humor	• Immature
• Adaptable	• Takes little seriously
• Energetic	• Attention-seeking
	• Can't focus

Beliefs That Drive Behavior

If I make people laugh they will like me.

If I make people laugh I won't feel my own pain.

If I make people laugh they won't feel their pain

Response to Feelings

Mask the pain.

Acting-Out Child

Acting-out children, the ones who were constantly in trouble, will continue to find conflicts in adulthood. They do not know how to feel good about themselves. They have been unable to interact with others in acceptable ways and have been unable to express their own needs or have them met. They were always aware of their anger but seldom aware of other feelings.

> I spent most of my years dominated with anger and resentment. I transferred my pain by fighting someone, anyone. I didn't care if I won or lost. I would fight with words. I would fight with my fists. I was blind to the consequences. Fighting was a way of releasing negative feelings dammed up inside. It gave me a way, at least for a moment, to feel I had some power over my life force. It was energy. It compensated for the nothingness.

Children usually gravitate toward others with similar personality traits to form a peer group. Some identify more as loners. If they had spent time in the justice system or psychiatric institutions, they often continue this pattern.

Upon reaching adulthood, acting-out children find their behavior (or lack of it) has caused significant problems. This behavior now complicates their adult lives because they may lack a high school education, frequently challenge authority, do not contain their anger, possibly have an unplanned pregnancy, or have had youthful marriage and all of the problems that frequently come with that. It's often common that the acting-out child is the recovering addict who is reading this book. The sooner he or she gets into trouble, the sooner this child has the potential to get help. Yet these children have strengths often not tapped.

The following table notes the strengths and vulnerabilities common to the Acting-Out Child. Vulnerabilities pertain to emotional and psychological skills not learned due to the rigidity of the role.

Strengths	Vulnerabilities
• Close to own feelings • Less denial, greater honesty • Creative • Sense of humor • Ability to lead	• Inappropriate expressions of anger • Inability to follow direction • Intrusive • Social problems at young ages (truancy, addiction, high school dropout, teen pregnancy, etc.)

Beliefs That Drive Behavior

If I scream enough, someone may notice me.

Take what you want. No one is going to give you anything.

Response to Feelings

I am angry about it, whatever it is.

Mixing and Matching Roles

Some children clearly fit into one or more of these roles. For most though, there are both primary and secondary roles.

Jon described himself predominantly as the responsible child, but during times of violence in his home he moved into the adjusting role. Since he was young, he believed he needed to take the pressure off his mother. His father seldom worked and would spend his days away from home. Neither his mother nor the kids knew how their father occupied his time. Jon took it upon himself to take charge of keeping the house clean and seeing that his brother and sister were kept entertained while his mother worked ten to twelve hours a day. On a daily basis, it was Jon who created order in the home. After school he would walk to where his mother worked, get money to go to the grocery store, get dinner ready, clean up the house, and see that his brother and sister did their homework. He didn't allow himself to feel any stress that would naturally be associated to this.

His father talked a lot about working, but Jon doesn't really remember his dad having any steady jobs. Jon was a good student, bringing pride to his father. He can remember listening to his father brag about him to his using buddies. Over the years his father's behavior at home became frightening as he was increasingly intoxicated and loaded. He frequently accused the children of liking their mother more than him. His paranoia was often sexual in nature—being suspicious of his wife, accusing her of sexual affairs, accusing his daughter of being sexual with boys. His inappropriate behavior would escalate and he would become verbally abusive, frequently lying and, ultimately, become physically violent, often threatening to kill the whole family.

Jon described the incredible fear he felt as his father began to take siege in their home. Jon said there was no illusion of his power. All he knew at these times was it was best to lie low, become invisible. Do not draw any attention to himself, disappear into the woodwork if possible. At such times, it was everyone for themselves. Not because he wasn't concerned about his siblings and mother but to do anything was provocation to his father.

While those frightening times lasted only from minutes to hours, it was the intensity, not the duration, that created the impact. Jon would move from being the responsible child to the adjuster in a literal fight for survival. Decades later, at times when he would feel frightened, he would again depart from being a capable, responsible adult and feel as if he were twelve years old and responding to the terror of his father's threats all over again. Jon is in an adult body. But on the inside he feels like a helpless frightened child. His body remembers the terror.

Shannon described herself as mostly acting-out, but within her group of peers she became a placater. At home she was blatantly angry and often sullen. She talked back to her mother and was verbally abusive to her sister. In junior high she was sneaking out of the house to be with friends. She performed poorly in school, not paying much attention and frequently skipping classes by high school. But when she was with her friends she wanted only to please them. She created and was a part of the conflict at home, but in her peer group she frequently did what she could to keep peace among her friends. It was with her friends that she had a greater sense of being a part of, of belonging. Shannon didn't understand what was happening at home and did not feel valued. With her friends, however, there was a way for her to be accepted.

Noah is like many mascots, in that this role often is combined with being an acting-out child. Being the youngest in the family, he quickly became the family pet. His arrival seemed a welcome distraction from what was happening in the family. As he got older, he thrived in the attention his humor brought to his siblings and to his mother. His addict father didn't find Noah's wit and energy to be endearing as much as annoying. But as he moved into his teenage years, Noah's high energy, his inability to focus on what was being asked of him at school, and his family starting to scatter, all created a situation where his humor was no longer a source of connection and validation. He started to hang out with kids who did appreciate his humor and soon he used his brightness and wit to do things that in the beginning were small pranks. He was desperate for attention, desperate to be acknowledged. Pressured to take risks that initially broke rules at school, then laws, gave him a stronger identity. Being a mascot and acting-out child are a natural combination, both roles distract others from the real issues at home, both draw attention to self, and in both roles they often find a peer group that appreciates their antics.

A percentage of children will change and adopt different roles as they grow older. They tend to do this as their environment changes, and they find the old role no longer serves its purpose or a new role creates greater security. Erica would move from being the responsible/placater to acting-out as her initial roles simply no longer worked for her. She was helping to raise her three younger brothers. Her mother was loaded most of the time. After a while the responsibilities became too great and her efforts seemed futile. Her brothers were no longer obeying her. She started to stay away from home. When home, she was frustrated with the different men who kept coming in acting as if they were her dad and then taking charge of the family. Ultimately, she began to hang out on the streets. The placater disappeared, and the ability to take charge, to initiate, and organize would redirect itself in her acting out and becoming a leader on the streets.

Both of Ronnie's parents were addicts. His mother was addicted to pills and alcohol and his father was hooked on a combination of drugs and alcohol. He was the third child, and his two brothers were four and six years older than he. He always relied on his older brothers, and they took good care of him. He doesn't remember a lot about his early childhood but describes it mostly as seeing his brothers as his parents. They dressed him. They saw to it that he went to school. When he was in grade school he can remember one of them meeting him at school and walking him home every day for a couple of years. His father wasn't around much of the time. When his dad was home he was mostly quiet and aloof. The older brothers also took care of their mother. He described the situation as one where it was as if his mother needed her own parent to tell her what she had to do, such as getting dressed, eating, maybe signing papers for school, or seeing that certain bills were paid. If anything, Ronnie described himself as a placater, wanting to please his older brothers. When the two older brothers left the home, he was just thirteen. "There was no one there to take care of Mom and she was in no shape to take care of herself most of the time, so I took over that role. It was not so much that I was trying to please her, I just moved into the responsible parenting role to keep her alive and I guess a place for me to stay."

By the time I was eleven I had begun to confront my parents and tried to act as a mediator in their fights. I became the caretaker, the people pleaser, and the scapegoat. I had to take on all of these roles because there was only one of me. I'd switch into whatever role I thought would solve the situation.

I became everything to everyone. I could be the perfect child, I made good grades, I was popular, I ordered the groceries, did the dishes. I made both my parents laugh. I was needed! Still, I was never sure when I came home if I was the selfish brat or the adored child."

There are strengths and deficits with each role children adopt. Unfortunately, because the skills developed within the roles are often acquired from a basis of fear and shame, they become extreme ways of coping and reacting. These coping behaviors also fuel problems due to undeveloped skills. It is vital to know how to initiate, but if you do not learn how to follow, it creates problems when you need to relate to others. It is good to be flexible, but if you never learn to make an autonomous decision, you risk victimization or never having your needs met. It is important to stand up for your rights and own your anger, but if you cannot identify other feelings, you lose the opportunity for intimacy. Self-reliance is a wonderful virtue but, at the price of never trusting others, it creates painful isolation. The key to healing is in finding balance.

Fueling Addiction

Studies have also shown that addiction repeats itself within the family from generation to generation. Overall, the results of many biological studies indicate that children of alcoholics react differently to alcohol or other drugs because of a difference in biochemical transmission. The research suggests:

- Children of alcoholics may suffer chemical imbalances that make them prone to substance-abusing behaviors.
- Children of alcoholics have increased feelings of pleasure and relaxation from alcohol ingestion, increased elation and/ or decreased muscle tension in response to alcohol ingestion, decreased feelings of intoxication at the same blood alcohol levels compared with children of nonalcoholics, and a possible serotonergic deficiency or an exaggerated level of serotonin when ingesting alcohol.

This does not mean that if they drink they will become alcoholic; it means the brain chemistry is such that there is a far greater likelihood due to the biological vulnerability. It is estimated that genetics account for 40–60 percent of the risk of the development of alcohol abuse or dependence. Environmental factors also play a serious role.

While it is common for children who recognize they are being raised with substance use disorders to say they will not drink or use when they get older, in reality, most of them choose to do so. They begin drinking and using at about the same ages and for the same reasons that children from nonaddicted families make similar choices. These youngsters usually begin to drink in their early teens. Like their peers, they drink to have fun because their friends want them to or out of curiosity or defiance. They drink to feel grown up; they drink to escape. Most teenagers typically drink just to get drunk. They are experimenting. But most significantly, they drink with an added belief—*it will never happen to me*. They may recognize their parent is addicted, but they believe that addiction is based on a lack of willpower, that it is a control issue. This belief says, "I have seen enough and I know enough about what alcohol and drugs can do to a person. I will be different."

For a child who has grown up with confusion, fear, shame, and powerlessness, alcohol and other drugs offer more than what they offer young people from healthier families. While it is often perceived that the angry, acting-out child is the one more likely to choose alcohol and other drugs as an escape, these substances offer answers and become a solution to any child of addiction regardless of family role.

As I describe the emotional and psychological influences specific to the different roles, I will use alcohol as the drug of choice knowing that for most people who become addicted their use begins with alcohol. Yet, it is also common that children, in an attempt to make sure they do not repeat the patterns of their parent(s), resort to a different substance or behavior to meet their needs. If it is not alcohol or other drugs, it is often food, spending/shopping, gambling, screen time, gaming, or sex. People who have process addictions will find that specific behaviors they engage in are reinforced in a similar manner. Whatever your drug of choice, it gives you something you didn't get to learn or experience, and you engage more and more to get the desired effect. As far as the brain is concerned a reward is a reward, regardless of whether it comes from a substance, behavior, or experience.

Responsible Child

For the responsible child, alcohol helps him loosen up and relax. When he drinks, he isn't quite as serious. Although these same personality changes occur in most people who drink, for those who are stuck in unhealthy patterns, alcohol may be the only thing that provides relief. Taking a drink makes them feel adequate—a feeling that to be sustained leads from one drink to another and then another. When these individuals drink, they are able to become more open with their feelings, show some vulnerability, and discover that other people respond to them more positively when they exhibit this relaxed and open manner. This does not necessarily make them addicted, but it does reinforce their need to drink and sets them up for a psychological dependency.

> I was this perfect kid. Academically, I did well and got a lot of satisfaction from being a part of the "in" group. I belonged. I had the right girlfriend. My family looked good to the outsiders. But by the time I went to college, I was emotionally numb, confused, but wasn't looking back. I had seen enough alcohol to float a small country. But excessive drinking made drinking seem normal to me. So when I began to have a drink every night before going to bed, it didn't strike me that no one else in the dorm had a drink every night or took a bottle of vodka with them to classes or put liquor in a mouthwash bottle. I drank to relax, to relieve pain, to hide from alienation and vague feelings of anxiety. But mostly to get rid of, to hide, or to mask the way I felt. It was also the time in which I felt closest to my dad.

Adjuster

For adjusters, alcohol removes feelings of inadequacy while giving them a sense of power. This is a false sense of power, but if you have felt only powerlessness in your life false power feels better than no power. Under the influence they may find themselves aware of undiscovered options and alternatives. Making decisions becomes easier, as does experiencing honest feelings and talking about the real issues. With this newfound power comes increased self-confidence. In order to maintain these feelings it is necessary to have another drink and another, and yet another. Ultimately, alcohol provides a state of being that feels good. It becomes a way of experiencing feelings that can't seem to be felt except with the use of alcohol. Again, it sets them up for a psychological dependency.

> *I loved alcohol from the first swallow. I had been a time bomb waiting to explode. I had finally found a way to connect, to be a part of. It fixed me, something to make me feel adequate, okay, and able to cope.*

Placater

Alcohol performs wonders for many placaters. Drinking helps them to focus more on themselves rather than others. Initially, this is very scary and they feel guilty but with a bit more to drink or use that guilt lessens. They are finding it feels good to focus on themselves. They no longer feel the weight of the world they have carried on their shoulders due to taking care of so many others. Using allows placaters to become more assertive. It empowers them to be more honest about their feelings. Instead of the perpetual smile, they are more real. Again, this too is scary and with more to drink or use they forget that fear and enjoy this newfound freedom. Ultimately, drinking becomes the solution to a problem they didn't even recognize. Before long, the psychological trap of dependency has become a reality.

> *I wasn't a happy child. I was always trying to make sure I was liked. I tried so hard to please everyone. It was tiring. I remember being thirteen and at a girlfriend's house and a bunch of us were drinking screwdrivers. I was walking home and noticing that my lip was numb. I thought it felt wonderful and I wished that I could always feel that way. And then I started to smoke pot and thought this stuff is great for me. I saw the world in a whole different light.*

It wasn't long before I was using pot almost every day. I used it to maintain. Then I drank for total oblivion.

Mascot

Being a comic is cute when you are young or in adulthood when it is an attribute versus the essence of your identity. As you grow older and need to take on personal responsibility, mascots may not get the reinforcement they once did. When that attention begins to wane they are left with their pain. Loneliness and fear are their more predominant emotional experiences. Alcohol and other drugs are often the answer. Because mascots often find the same benefits acting out, using and drinking are quick solutions to the pain they have been running from since a young age.

Oh I was a funny kid. Even I found myself funny. But other kids became tired of it I guess and they let me know I needed to grow up. I couldn't grow up. It hurt too bad. So I laughed my way into a peer group that tolerated what I guess was childishness on my part. But it simply was the humor and antics I had always used. I can remember my first drink; it was really my first drunk. I got up on top of a car, took off part of my clothes, and did what I thought was a comic routine. I made a name for myself. But I found I needed the alcohol to get that out of control. But at least I still had an audience. At least someone still noticed me.

Acting-Out Child

Using alcohol and other drugs is the typical trademark of rebellion. Substances allows people to feel better about themselves, giving them a false sense of confidence in their abilities. It's a way of saying to the world "you will notice me," while it drowns their pain. It is also a way for them to feel they have power in the face of a sense of defeat and hopelessness about their lives. This child typically begins drinking at a younger age than kids in other roles and, as a result, moves quickly to abuse and develops his or her addiction at earlier ages with rapid progression. The flip side of this is theoretically they are more likely to be directed to help earlier as they are getting into trouble so young.

At age forty-six, Patty is still acting out her anger. She was an angry teenager and has been an angry adult. Despite having a college degree, her addiction has blocked her career, and she has resorted to supporting herself as a bartender. Patty has been married three times. She has relinquished the parenting of her children to the different fathers. Known for her belligerent attitude, Patty has challenged nearly everyone in authority positions, from her bosses to police. As a result, few people welcome her presence in their lives today.

> I began to use and drink when I was about twelve. I was so angry and was always in trouble, and in the beginning it calmed me down. It made it easier to get along with friends. I was already out of the house as much as I could be. It didn't take long until it seemed I just got into more trouble, but I didn't care. I had found something to fix me, something to fill up the horrible empty hole.

Joseph summarized it all by saying, "I could play any role. I played them one right after another, never knowing who I was and never being me. I hated the insanity and the abuse in my family. Everything was out of control. The whole thing was nuts and I hated it—my mother's hysteria, my father's drinking. I wanted to kill myself, but never got the courage, so I let alcohol and drugs do it for me."

A good guideline: any time you use a substance or become involved in a process or behavior that interferes with your honesty or the ability to be present with yourself, it deserves your attention.

CHAPTER FIVE

Living with Trauma

Children of addiction are also children of trauma. It would be several years after the initial writing of *It Will Never Happen to Me* that people's responses to acute trauma, such as a shooting, a car accident, a natural disaster, and acts of terrorism would be studied in depth. With the focus of research on people's responses to traumatic incidents, it became apparent post-traumatic stress that was identified during the Vietnam war was being experienced by people who had different traumas. As researchers and psychotherapists were becoming more familiar with post-traumatic stress, they noticed that the trauma responses they witnessed in those who were survivors of acute trauma were many of the same responses occurring in people with chronic stressful childhoods. Children raised with addiction experience what is called *developmental trauma* as they are subjected to both traumatic stress and acute traumas during their developmental years—the time in their life when their bodies, brains, and personalities are being formed.

When a family is ill with the disease of addiction, its members are much more likely to experience trauma than those from nonaddicted families. Addiction worsens every dimension of trauma.

Addiction creates chronic losses for everyone in the family—a loss of trust, connection, intimacy, stability, honesty, fun, clear communication, safety, and healthy boundaries. As the disease progresses, family members also lose jobs, relationships, financial stability, and health. Some lose their lives. Not having the opportunity to grow up outside the veil of fear and shame, children lose the innocence of their childhoods. As one loss gets compounded upon another, the result is trauma.

Basic Facts about Trauma

- Trauma is caused by an event that the body and parts of the brain perceive as overwhelming or terrifying.
- Trauma breaks down one's psychological defenses and shatters one's sense of security.
- Most events that cause trauma are unexpected. Yet, for many in a family impacted by addiction, they do expect it, they just don't always know when.
- Trauma can be the result of a string of expected but unavoidable painful events, repeated over and over. This is even more descriptive of life with addiction in the family.
- Many traumas occur in the context of relationships. When the source of that trauma is someone who is supposed to care for you, love you, support you, the impact is greater.

Children demonstrate differences in their responses to trauma due to three important factors:

1. Their age at the time the trauma occurs or begins. The younger you are as you begin to experience traumatic stress, the greater the biological impact as it is impinging on the whole body in its crucial development. Unfortunately, many children are born into families already experiencing the impact of addiction in the family.

2. The help that others provide or fail to provide during or after a traumatic event will have a profound effect on how well and how quickly you recover. Children who had a parent who offered some protection and nurturing in spite of what was occurring in the family will benefit. Many children can credit other siblings for protecting and nurturing them. Frequently, extended family members such as grandparents, or someone at school (a particular teacher or coach), or often a friends' parent, will have a positive impact on a child. Many adult children are able to identify a host

of people throughout their lives who they will credit with offering some support. Having someone or a combination of people in your life who helps you feel cared for, loved, helps with problem-solving, or simply gives you a respite or encouragement is extremely important in helping you develop resiliency in the face of trauma. They become your safety net.

3. The more previous traumas you have experienced the greater the traumatic impact. Trauma placed upon already existing trauma accumulates and the stress has a multiplying effect. A soldier who experiences trauma in combat is more likely to have post-traumatic stress if he or she also experienced traumatic stress growing up. If there are two girls being bullied at school and one is raised in a family impacted by addiction and the other is not, the one raised with addiction will struggle even more with the impact of the bullying. If your mother is ill with a terminal illness while you are growing up in an addicted house that will increase the traumatic stress. The stress that comes with having one parent who is bipolar, having difficult mood swings, and a second parent who is addicted reinforces the traumatic responses. When the trauma accumulates, the impact of trauma is amplified. Knowing this helps you understand why it is you may have more or less resiliency than another person raised with addiction. It also explains why some people need additional resources in their recovery plan. Identifying with multiple issues is more common than not.

In addition to addressing the vulnerabilities that come with the family roles and rules, recognizing the trauma will offer a better overall understanding of the impact of addiction.

Emotional Abandonment Continuum

The most prevalent form of trauma is emotional abuse, which can take any or all of these forms:

- Severe criticism and blaming.
- Verbal abuse.

- Broken promises.
- Lying.
- Unpredictability.
- Rage.
- Harsh or even cruel forms of punishment.
- Being forced into physically dangerous situations such as being in a vehicle with an impaired driver.

Emotional trauma can be more subtle, it is also:
- Parental indifference to a child's needs and wants.
- Emotional unavailability, not showing love and concern.
- Unrealistic expectations, having expectations that are not age-appropriate due to not having the ability or skills. For example, expecting the eight-year-old to remember his or her dental appointment, expecting the ten-year-old to be responsible for the two-month old sibling, or expecting a child to do something he or she can't physically do. I've heard many stories of kids being challenged to engage in an athletic event that is far beyond their ability or to do yard work that ultimately takes a team of people or mechanical equipment to be able to perform the job.
- Your worth or value as a person is not separated out from your actions. Disapproval is aimed at your entire being, your identity rather than a particular behavior. This may involve being told that you are worthless when you have not done your homework or that you are never going to be a good athlete because you missed the final catch of the game.
- Boundary violation or distortion. This happens when:
  - Parents do not view children as separate beings from themselves wanting the children to meet their needs.
  - Parents are not willing to take responsibility for their feelings, thoughts, and behaviors but expect the child to take responsibility for them.
  - Parents' self-esteem is derived totally through their child's behavior.

- Children are treated as peers with no parent-child distinction.
- Parents expect children to fulfill their dreams.
- Parents objectify children as possessions or belongings versus as their own human entity with rights and desires.

When parents are disrespectful and violate a child's boundaries, the message given is that they don't value the child as a person. That message becomes internalized as "I am not of value. I am not worthy." When parents don't acknowledge a child's boundaries, the message they give is "You are here to meet my needs, not me yours " and/or "I am more important than you" and/or "It is not okay to be your own person with individual feelings, desires, or needs." The message also implies that the children have to give up themselves to be available to another person. This results in the internalized belief "I am bad for having different or separate needs, wants, and feelings."

You can identify abandonment as occurring when you realize that you have to hide a part of yourself in order to be accepted or to avoid rejection. Those parts you learn to hide are:

- Mistakes. To make a mistake or to be less than perfect draws punitive responses.
- Feelings. Being told the way you feel is not true or okay. "You have nothing to cry about and if you don't stop crying I will really give you something to cry about." "That really didn't hurt." "You have nothing to be angry about." This is not about the occasional time a parent becomes frustrated with a child and makes such a comment but an ongoing pattern of parenting.
- Needs. Everyone else's needs appear to be more important than yours; and the only way you get attention is by attending to the needs of others.
- Successes. Accomplishments are not acknowledged, are many times discounted, or even used as ammunition to shame a child.

Sometimes it seems as if I was abandoned emotionally. Other times it feels as if I was never claimed in the first place.

Physical Abandonment Continuum

I didn't question all of the drinking because I had to spend so much time responding to the abuse.

Physical abandonment includes physical and sexual abuse, as well as neglect. While most children of addiction will experience emotional abandonment, some will experience the combination of both emotional and physical abandonment.

Because people who have been raised in abusive families have a high tolerance for inappropriate behavior and violence, it is often helpful to describe abusive behavior.

When we think of physical abuse, we often picture a badly beaten, chronically black-and-blue child. In reality, battering may be much more subtle and infrequent, with barely visible results. Battering can occur in the form of pushing and shoving, grabbing, pinching, or choking. It may be slapping, hitting, kicking, punching, or slamming a person against the wall, to the floor, against the car.

Yet, in many addictive homes, only terror exists; no bruises attesting to violence are evident. Children and partners frequently experience intensely frightening and physically dangerous situations. When Dad, in a drunken siege, takes the family for a sixty-miles-per-hour car ride down a mountain road at night with the headlights turned off, the effect is just as traumatic as any physical violence, yet it leaves no physical scars.

Michael describes his mother's rages, "I can still see my mom throwing dishes, and I can hear her yelling at us kids things we should never have heard."

We never knew when he would blow up, or for what, and who would be the target of his anger. He would suddenly threaten one of us for no reason at all. His favorite saying was, "This is my house, and I'll do what I want."

We never really knew what provoked them. They were quick to raise their voices or hit us. Mom would pick a fight with me out of nowhere and hit me. We could be doing something that we had done lots of times without them ever saying anything and then the next time we'd do it, they'd notice and we'd get hit for it. If you didn't do the dishes right, you could get hit. It never made sense.

The trauma is in the witnessing of abuse directed toward others in the family that is often more damaging than receiving the abuse itself.

I would be terrified. The voices were loud, and sometimes my stepmother would throw things. I pretended I heard nothing. I would be terrified that something awful would happen. Sometimes the police would come, sometimes the neighbors.

My father would always beat my mother when he was drunk. Then he got so he beat my brother. I hated it. Then I got so I tried to interfere and be a referee to prevent the arguing that would lead to the violence. But one night he threw me onto a chair, told me to shut up or I'd get the bottle right across my face. I tried to speak up but quickly shut up. He would have done it. After that, I could only watch. I hated him, but even more I hated me for my powerlessness and fear.

What actually goes on in the day-to-day existence of a child who lives in the shadow of physical violence is often beyond the imagination of those who have never had such an experience.

When Dad drank, someone got beat. We hated to see him get started, but the quarreling was awful loud. My mom was hurt a lot. How did he get started on me? Simple. I defended my mom and if he wanted to know who did something, rather than see my younger brother or sisters get it, I did it! No matter what it was. He usually used a Marine belt on us. I still look out for my brother and sisters and my mom; I wouldn't lift a finger to help my dad. I refused to go to his funeral or send flowers. I am the same with my own kids, take care of them, protect them from my ex-husband, who somehow has managed to develop a dependency on prescription drugs, always has a beer in his hand, and likes to hit.

Andrea has a similar story: "My mother taught me that at all costs I should never do anything to make my father angry. I lived in constant fear of his awful silence that could at the most unexpected moment turn into a red-faced rage. I have a mental picture of myself in a crouch, like a dog that looks pleadingly, hoping not to be beaten up, but expecting it, hoping to please the master but knowing it will never happen. The master will not—cannot—be pleased."

When caretakers don't provide safety in our environment, we grow up believing that the world is an unsafe place, that people are not to be trusted, and that we do not deserve positive attention and adequate care. This way of life becomes a legacy that we accept, not knowing how to make it different.

Similarities of the Abuser and the Addict

While addiction and battering are not always related, it is helpful to examine similarities in the dynamics of both. When they coexist and interact, the dynamics are multiplied.

Both the batterer and the addict:

- Minimize and deny their abusive behaviors.
- Discount their acts and minimize the severity of their drunkenness or battering.
- Blame others; neither will accept the responsibility for their behavior.
- Exhibit Jekyll-and-Hyde personality changes. Children may experience an overly nice, caring parent who after taking a few drinks becomes a raging lion. In this case, the batterer simply erupts like a volcano for what appears to be no apparent reason.
- Rationalize their behavior and, invariably, there is (in their own rationale) a good reason (excuse) for the drinking or for the violent behavior. Episodic violence and drinking occur more and more frequently as these unhealthy lifestyles progress. Inevitably, for the addicted and the batterer, the using and the violence begin to cause more trauma and more problems in almost all areas of family and personal life.
- Increasingly feel more guilt and remorse.
- Make promises and create false hopes.
- Continue this cycle indefinitely unless they seek help.

Partners and children:

- Minimize the impact of the drinking and/or using and violence in the family. This is the family's denial process. The dysfunctional family rules of Don't Feel, Don't Trust, and Don't Talk permeate the family. Addiction, when coupled with violence, doubles the need for denial and creates an even greater sense of helplessness in the lives of family members. When children don't show obvious signs of being emotionally affected by violence, it is important to recognize that it is probably due to denial. Children in battered families develop an almost identical denial process as the children

in addictive homes. When addiction and battering coexist, they
practice denial to a greater extent.
- Accept the blame because they believe that had they been better in
  their roles (a better wife or a better child) the batterer/addict would
  have no reason to get so upset, fly into rages, and drink or use.

Children are naturally vulnerable. They have no frame of reference
from which they can make judgments and tend to believe anything they
are told. Their own sense of confusion makes them quick to accept blame
for any given situation. They feel powerless in dealing with grown-ups, see
themselves as not having the available resources, and unable to protect
themselves.

Role patterns in the violent home are often similar to those seen in
addictive homes, only with an even greater intensity when both problems
coexist. There is one significant difference between homes plagued with
addiction and those with violence. Addiction usually manages to reveal
itself to others outside the home, whereas family violence is much more
hidden from those not living in the home. The goal of family members
in attempting to live through these problems is the same—minimize the
conflict, adjust, placate, act out, drop out—do anything just to survive.

Sexual Abuse Continuum

*I am apprehensive talking about this problem because I am afraid
others might find out. I was seven when my dad began to touch
me and make me touch and kiss him. He did a lot of things to me.
It hurt. He used to threaten me that he would do the same thing
to my younger sisters if I told. I didn't know what to do when I was
eighteen so I stayed home another year. He died in a drinking-and-
driving accident. Then I left home, never telling anyone. Years later
I found out he had been molesting my sisters all of that time, too.
I am only now beginning to accept my past and present family
situations. I withdraw from people when afraid because I think
they might hurt me. I don't visit my mother or sisters. I feel guilty
for never going home. I've always felt guilty.*

Child sexual abuse is a form of child abuse that includes sexual activity with a minor. It does not need to include physical contact between a perpetrator and a child. Types of child sexual abuse include:

- Fondling.
- Intercourse.
- Sex of any kind with a minor, including vaginal, oral, or anal.
- Masturbation in the presence of a minor or forcing the minor to masturbate.
- Sexually explicit phone calls, text messages, other digital screen interactions.
- Creating, owning, or sharing pornographic images or movies of children.
- Sex trafficking.
- Exhibitionism or exposing oneself to a minor.
- Any other sexual conduct that is harmful to a child's mental, emotional, or physical welfare.

Sexual abuse is inappropriate sexual behavior, usually perpetrated by an adult with a minor child—male or female—and brought about by coercion, deception, or psychological manipulation.

While research concerning sexual abuse and its relationship to addictive disorders continues to be limited, both physical and sexual abuse are three times more likely to be perpetrated by a parent with a substance use disorder. That does not take into account the nonaddicted person in a parental role, siblings, or other extended family members who could be the perpetrator. About two thirds of incest perpetrators report using alcohol directly before the offending incident. Should both parents be addicted to substances, the likelihood of both parents being perpetrators is more common, and while both females and males could be abused, the likelihood of males being abused increases when parents are addicted. Due to the possibility of greater neglect when both parents are addicted, the likelihood of sexual abuse by people outside of the family also increases.

Perpetrators seldom commit childhood sexual abuse to solely satisfy their own sexual needs. It is an act of violence and selfishness, and it is a violation of a position of trust, power, and protection—and it thrives in silence. Abusers use power, age, experience, and position to persuade, coerce, bribe, and threaten their victims into doing things they are not old enough or emotionally mature enough to cope with or defend against. The perpetrator takes advantage of the child's emotional, social, or financial dependence on him or her. If the person who becomes sexual with the child is even just a few years older than the child or holds a position of power or authority, it is *molestation*; if the person is related to the child it is *incest*. Both constitute sexual abuse.

Even if the victim doesn't try to stop it, the child is not responsible for the sexual abuse. Remember, a child who is the victim of sexual abuse usually has no place to escape to and is too frightened to tell. Children are too young and immature to make the kinds of decisions that are involved in this type of sexual behavior. It is the responsibility and the fault of the older, more powerful person.

Silence Is Survival

Children don't talk about the sexual abuse for many of the same reasons they don't talk about the addiction.

So many times, the onset is very gradual and children may not even recognize what is happening until the behavior has been repeated for some time. By then, children are scared and ashamed.

Not trusting your own feelings is experienced at an early age in an addictive family. Knowing feelings helps you to know your needs, to be able to speak up. Feelings are cues and signals. So when they are not trusted, a child will be more immobilized.

If the child challenges the appropriateness of the perpetrator's behavior he or she is manipulated into feeling guilty for questioning the molester's actions or may possibly be threatened. The child begins to believe his or her perceptions are faulty so he or she will succumb to the demands. The youngster then becomes intimidated and readily assumes the guilt and responsibility.

> I didn't tell anybody about it. I was about eight when it started. I had a vague idea it was something bad, but I didn't know what sex was.

I only knew the way he acted was something I didn't want to be part of. I would try to avoid getting into those situations. I would come home from school late hoping Mom would get home first. I made up excuses not to go places alone with him. But, once it began, I just sort of passively sat there. I wouldn't talk to him, and when he let me go, I would get out of there as quickly as possible. I never told anyone what he was doing. Oftentimes, when he came into my bedroom, I thought if I pretended I was asleep he would go away, and I really didn't want to acknowledge that it was happening.

In addition, children fear they will not be believed if they tell. That could well be true, for this is already a family where telling the truth is not supported. People in the addictive family are busy rationalizing and minimizing hurtful, neglectful, or inappropriate behavior. People are not held accountable for their behavior and blaming is more common. But as another survivor said, "She wouldn't have done anything about it anyway. That might have hurt more, and that would kill me."

It is not uncommon to hear of a sexual abuse survivor who has told a parent and that parent reacts punitively, as if the child is putting one more burden on the parent to handle. It is easier to blame a child and accuse him or her of looking for attention and lying than to face something that seems so overwhelming and shameful. Unfortunately, the dynamics of the family are often such that the needs of the adult supersede the needs of the child. There is often immaturity of a parent that doesn't allow him or her to listen, prioritize the needs of, or protect his or her child.

Another adult child revealed, "I do remember being really scared, like I shouldn't be doing this—but he was my father. You listen to your father. I did it because he wanted me to do it; it was expected of me. You don't argue in my family. No one has rights in my family until you are out of the house and self-supporting."

Victims are often afraid the family will break up if they don't go along with what the perpetrator wants. The addictive family is already on such shaky ground that children are terrified of losing the little stability they still have. They feel that if the family were to break up they would be responsible for it.

If this weren't enough, the perpetrator often threatens to hurt or even kill the victim, another family member, or a pet if the child tells about the abuse. These are children who already feel false guilt for the conflict or unspoken pain in the family. This is just one more threatening consequence of asking for help or telling the truth.

It is also common for victims to become confused about the abuse when they were not physically forced to comply. Perpetrators often play on trust to coerce their victim into meeting their demands. It is well known that abusers often choose children starving for attention, warmth, and affection. Children from troubled families are prime victims because they are particularly desperate for any sign of attention and affection. Kaylie described her stepfather as the only father she knew. Her biological father had no contact with the family. Her stepfather was the primary parent in the family. He frequently fixed the dinner and helped the children with their homework, while her mother was often at school, out with friends, or simply not wanting to do those things at home. So when he began to give her long hugs and then back rubs, it seemed to be just another way of his attending to her. When he ultimately wanted her to touch him sexually, she said she was not scared, it was just being nice to him for being so good to her.

When Dan's molestation began at the age of ten, he said he also liked the attention he was getting from the man who was the offender. He said his friend's father took him to ball games and gave him money. He also reported that the molestation not only didn't hurt, but it physically felt good. At home he didn't know when his dad would be raging next. His father never affectionately touched him or said anything nice to him so he gravitated to the father figure who showed him attention.

Sexual abuse is an insidious type of violence that often does not require physical force. However, that does not mean the victim wanted it to happen. Kaylie and Dan wanted affection and attention. That is understandable. And perpetrators prey on such children to manipulate and seduce. Survivors of sexual abuse are also confused if the experience has any physical pleasure associated with it. Having physical pleasure is a biological response, and it in no way implies being complicit. Some boys will have an erection or ejaculate during an assault, which they find confusing. Again, that is a physiological response and does not imply the child wanted or invited the assault. Should the abuse be coupled with any other gains, such as Dan's experience of getting attention from a man who appeared to like him versus a father who raged at him, it makes it less likely he would recognize this as abusive. He would be less likely to say stop, less likely to let another responsible adult know. But remember you were the child, they are the adult. They know what they are doing is wrong and hurtful. Neither Kaylie nor Dan realized they were being taken advantage of; they did not initially realize they were being victimized.

Coupled with the manipulations of the perpetrator, children from addictive families are less able to defend themselves by reaching out and letting others know what is happening.

Because of the dynamics of growing up with addiction they:

- Have greater difficulty identifying their feelings.
- Have a greater fear in trusting their perceptions and trusting others.
- Are more confused about what constitutes appropriate boundaries.
- Have an existing base of shame as a result of living with the dynamics of addiction. Shame upon shame fuels powerlessness making it more difficult to reach out for help.
- Have a wall of denial about what is occurring in their life.
- The powerlessness experienced over their body is compounded by the powerlessness felt within the family.
- Have learned there is no safe place.
- Feel locked in because there is no way to confront the offender or be believed and protected. To confront implies shame, guilt, denial, abandonment and, possibly, physical violence.

Nativity

*Red hood drapes his black robe's back candles subdue the
sanctuary, Noel Noel, we sing.
At midnight he stands before us rolling down the words
"There was no room at the inn." Raising his arms, they
fold down then close. Fruitcake, poinsettias, fudge fill our
parsonage, cookies, cards, and packages for the minister and
his family.*

*His daughter's presents are not wrapped. Red tissue paper
rustles, their shadows argue against the wall his voice
commanding, "Hurry up." He's naked swilling clear vodka.
Sobbing she cries, "You'll wake her."
Silent night Holy night All is calm All is bright.
I will stay here in this closet until morning when they call me
to open my presents all the tags in her handwriting.*

Joan

Covert Sexual Abuse

Adults who abuse alcohol and other drugs are not going to be proper role
models for children, particularly during the time when healthy attitudes
regarding sexuality need to be learned. Drug-affected and impaired
parents often speak crudely or tease children inappropriately with sexual
innuendoes. In some homes, children are forced to deal with the drunken
nudity of a parent and/or parents and who make no attempt at maintaining
discreet sex lives. The children very often face these problems alone, in
silence, confused, and feeling needless shame. This is covert sexual abuse,
often referred to as *emotional sexual abuse*. It may also involve an adult
telling details about his or her sex life to a child, flirting, or being jealous
of his or her son or daughter having a romantic relationship. Covert abuse
occurs when daughters are treated like wives or girlfriends and sons are
treated like husbands or boyfriends. It includes inappropriate touching

that appears to be accidental, a parent's habit of walking into the bathroom while a child or teenager is showering, or seductive comments about a child's developing body.

Lisa discussed her adolescent fears of believing she would be sexually violated. She was so sure of the possibility she had begun to take a knife to her bedroom to defend and protect herself from an anticipated attack.

She described her confusion as a result of the increasing change in behavior evidenced by her father. He changed from a caring, fun-loving father to a blaming, harsh, verbally abusive, drunken stranger. Lisa became more fearful of her father's actions when, along with his alcohol-induced behavior, he began talking about how girls who were sexual were bad. Then he would become graphic in his descriptions of women being sexual, and began accusing his daughters and his wife of sexually acting out. He demonstrated growing hostility toward Lisa and her sister's boyfriends. Eventually, he began visiting Lisa's room late at night to accuse her of sexual activity with boys. She knew her father was becoming sexually preoccupied with her, and her fear of possible sexual abuse by him coupled with the love she had felt for her dad led to a great sense of confusion and shame about her own sexuality. For three years, she took a knife to bed, hid it under a pillow, and took herself through a visualization where she let go of any positive feelings for her father and told herself she would kill him if he touched her. He never touched her. But she would carry the emotional scars of the terror and shame as well as the skill of dissociating from her feelings into her adult life.

Any abuse, from the covert to the most blatant, can wound a person's sense of self and sexuality. The damage includes feeling powerless, quickly succumbing to victimization, fear of being assertive, reluctance to trust, inability to stay mentally present during sex, fear of sex, shame about one's body, and fear of intimacy.

Assumptions

While childhood abuses often exist within addictive families, that does not mean one causes the other. Therefore, if the perpetrator is the addict, one cannot assume that should he or she stop using or drinking he or she will stop the abuse. Also, when the abusers are the addicted parent(s), abuse doesn't necessarily occur when they are drinking or using. In fact, some children report that the parent is more dangerous when not using or drinking. It also cannot be assumed that the addicted parent is the perpetrator of the abuse. The abusing parent may very well be the nonaddicted parent or another family member. When this is true, the addicted parent is so caught up in his or her disease that he or she is often oblivious to what is happening in a child's life or just too impaired to intervene.

> While Dad's drinking increased, Mom became more erratic. She was playful and fun one moment and full of rage the next. She would pick up anything (whip, vacuum cleaner hose, spoon) and hit and hit and hit, and would never apologize. Even when we were bleeding, somehow it was still our fault.

People often think of the perpetrators being the adults in a family; however, siblings may be the offenders. Brothers and sisters may terrorize each other, acting out their own frustrations, trying to find something to control and dominate in reaction to their helplessness, their anger, and their shame. They also often model what they see by adults. Lack of healthy supervision creates an environment of less protection. While not always, it is most likely the older children (regardless of gender) who become the abusers of the younger children in the home. The predominant model they have for their painful feelings is to attack someone less powerful.

Both sexual and physical abuse is an overwhelming, damaging, and humiliating assault on a child's mind, soul, and body.

Neglect

My parents didn't have to beat us; the neglect did it for them.

Neglect is another form of physical abandonment. It is when the physical conditions necessary for thriving do not exist. It is demonstrated with inadequate supervision, such as leaving young children in the care of other children nearly as young as them or leaving children with no supervision at all. Neglect is also inadequate physical care, such as not providing meals or proper clothing and shelter. Children describe never knowing when dinner is. "It could be anywhere from 6:00 p.m. to midnight. It would range from take-out food to hot dogs or ice cream."

Food was on a first-come, first-served basis. That meant I often went hungry because there was never enough food for us. We would grab from the stove and take it anywhere in the house. If our parents were really angry with us or really drunk, we didn't eat at all.

Children often have clothes that are too small or inadequate for the weather, such as thin coats or simply sweaters to withstand rain and snow. Neglect is also inadequate medical attention. Marti described, "My mother's way of coping was to ignore everything, thinking it would go away. She did this with both my diabetes and my father's violent rages."

The neglect may be so pervasive that children learn to not question or challenge it. For adult children, it is often only as they hear others talk and receive feedback that they begin to realize the extent of deprivation in their lives.

The neglect was okay, at least then they weren't deliberately hurting you.

With abuse of opiates, neglect is even more rampant. Greater number of children are living in poverty, don't have food, are not going to school, and are subject to dangers of drug paraphernalia laying around, and more likely to be the witness to overdoses and suicides. Children are frequently left to take care of each other. Parents are gone or simply too impaired to take responsibility for providing for their children.

We were left a lot with our older sister, but then she would leave too. We were mostly just three kids left alone. We tried not to be scared.

We never had the basics. We never had enough underwear or socks. We never had slippers. There was a major sense of being without. No one told us how to keep clean or how often. No one

*told us what to wear. One time the school called to have my sister
picked up and taken home to have a bath. We kids tried so hard.
We did our own laundry. We fixed our own food. We tried to keep
things orderly, but we had no space that was our own.*

Shame

Traumatic stress results in the child internalizing the belief that no matter
what he or she does it won't make a difference anyway, or no matter
what the child does, it's not good enough. Ultimately, that becomes
translated into the child believing he or she is not good enough. That is
the experience of shame.

*What are you supposed to think about yourself when the only
thing you were ever called growing up was stupid? Oh, if I didn't
get called stupid, I had a middle name, which was worthless.*

There are many words used that are descriptive of shame. The more
common words are when one thinks of him- or herself as stupid, bad,
dirty, damaged, defective, broken, a failure, or worthless.

Picture a wide-mouth funnel. As you are subjected to confusing and
painful experiences, you begin to take on the message that you are not
okay, not of value. The open end of the funnel is taking in a host of painful
feelings and negative messages. As the shame-based beliefs take hold, the
wide funnel becomes increasingly narrow. With a greater attachment to
the shame beliefs, the more disconnected you become from your feelings.
In recovery, as you challenge and let go of shame-based beliefs and develop
a healthier belief system, the narrow part starts to open up more widely
and the ability to feel will resume. In time, you come to embrace feelings
as friends not foes, cues to be listened to and valued.

In your growing-up years shame is regenerated over and over through
traumatic stress conditions. Shame is one of the most common and
pernicious responses to trauma and is carried long after the traumatic
events have occurred. It fuels every one of the pain responses discussed
in the next chapter.

CHAPTER SIX

Legacy of Family Trauma

At times of trauma, the natural response is to run, but not necessarily running from, as much as running to. Trauma survivors typically run toward home, but where do you go when the trauma is in your home?

When it is not safe psychologically or physically to be who you are, to own your truth, what you see, and how you feel, then you move into various trauma responses—you fight, you flee, or you freeze.

Your mother is standing over you, her face distorted in her anger, she's telling you she never wanted you in the first place. You are to stay out of her bedroom. The drugs are hers. She now is threatening to send you to live with your father who you don't even know. You are nine years old.

You witness your father hitting your older sister; he's raging at her and now threatening to hit your mother. In that moment, you hate him. You don't care that he just lost his job. You don't care that your mom says you are to be grateful for what you have. You hate him. And you hate yourself because you feel so powerless.

How can you fight back? Where can you flee to? Is your only option to freeze emotionally, to go numb inside?

The body cannot tell the difference between an emotional emergency and physical danger. When triggered, it responds by pumping out stress chemicals designed to impel you to quickly move to safety or enables you to stand and fight. In the case of childhood problems, where the family itself has become the source of stress, there may be no opportunity to fight or flee. So you do what you can. You freeze, shut down your inner responses by numbing or fleeing on the inside.

Your dad is loaded on his cocktail of drugs and is raging. A tired mom, one who used to try to protect you, now sits frozen on the living room couch. You want to run to the bedroom or outside but know that is a useless attempt. He'll just chase after you and get you. You want to scream you hate him and you know that will only make things worse. His rage could escalate and you and your brother who is also a witness to this could get hit, or maybe he would just tell you how worthless you both are. You just want to disappear. You remain standing but feel nothing, as if you just disappeared from yourself. You swallow the whole scene; the experience becomes embedded in your body and brain. This moment, this scene, gets added to the folder that holds all the previous ones. They all begin to blend together as you create a portrait of who you are.

The very people you want to flee from were those you needed and loved. The very people you should be able to go to for protection are the ones traumatizing you.

To live with fear on a chronic basis fuels ongoing traumatic stress, regardless of whether it is the consequence of more blatant or covert trauma. Without protection factors to override the impact of trauma, flight, fight, and freeze responses will be acted out.

Emotional Legacies of the Fight, Flight, and Freeze

Survival is about defending against your pain that aligns itself well with the fight, flight, and freeze responses. While the most apparent consequence of growing up with addiction is the generational repetition of becoming addicted and engaging in relationships with someone with addiction, even more common are the following trauma responses.

Control

Children learn to control in two ways: external and internal. The responsible child is often the master of external control, manipulating people, places, and things. This is the child who is the parent to brothers and sisters and to him- or herself. As Cam said, "I raised myself rather well." Tim set the bedtime for his younger brother and sister and made sure they had bathed and were tucked in. He made their lunches for school the next morning. Kimberly would call her father to tell him what he needed to do when he came home from work. All children are likely to try to control the internal, intangible aspect of their personal lives. They do that by withholding their feelings and diminishing their needs, neither expecting nor asking for anything.

- *I am not angry. What is there to be angry about?*
- *I wasn't embarrassed. I'm used to those things by now.*
- *I don't need to go to my friend's house. Who would be home to take care of my sister?*
- *I don't want a birthday party. My dad wouldn't show up anyway.*

This is self-control, protection to ward off further pain by repressing desires and feelings. As a child, the attempt to control internally or externally was about survivorship. It made sense in the context of your environment.

Unfortunately, the continued need for control causes problems in adult lives. You have spent years being hypervigilant and manipulating others as a way of protection. You literally don't know how to live life differently. Unfortunately, because of being so encapsulated and narrow in your view of the world, it's not possible to see what others can so readily see—that you have become authoritarian, demanding, inflexible, and perfectionistic.

Controllers don't know how to listen; cut people off in conversations; don't ask for help; can't see options; have little spontaneity; experience psychosomatic health problems; intimidate people by withholding feelings. Blindly focused on the pursuit of safety, very often unaware of your emotional self and yet so frightened and full of shame, you rely on what you know best—control. But the consequences are almost the opposite of what was hoped for. Your needs do not get met; relationships are out of balance. Ultimately, hypervigilance becomes burdensome and exhausting. In confusion about what has gone wrong when you have tried so hard to make things right, controllers resort to unhealthy ways of coping with pain that often results in addictive behaviors.

Perfectionism

While the issue of perfectionism may seem trite to some people, others wish they were more perfectionistic. Sadly, I have worked with many people who have attempted to take their lives in despair as their perfectionism has failed them. That ultimately has them concluding nothing they would ever do is good enough for them to be okay. Perfectionism is a major contributor to depression and anxiety.

Perfectionism is driven by the belief that if a person's behavior is perfect there will be no reason to be criticized and he or she can only be admired. And as well as children perform, often achieving lofty goals, perfect children have learned that no matter what they do, it's never good enough. As a result, in the struggle to feel good about themselves and relieve the source of pain, they constantly push to excel, to be the best at any cost. Yet there is always something missing once the goal is reached— there is always another goal, something more to complete.

Highly perfectionistic people are usually those who have been raised in a rigid home environment. The rigidity may be in the form of unrealistic expectations that parents have for their children. In these situations, you internalize your parents' expectations. Rigidity is also experienced as children feel the need to do things right in order to gain approval from their parent and to lessen fears of rejection. For most children, doing things right is perceived to mean there is no room for mistakes. What is then felt is that "no matter what I do, it's never good enough" and, for the young person, that becomes translated into "I am not good enough."

Children of addiction are taught to strive onward. There was never a time or place to rest or to have inner joy and satisfaction.

Perfection as a performance criterion means you can never measure up. Not measuring up is translated into a comparison with others of good versus bad, better versus worse. Inevitably, you end up feeling the lesser for the comparison. This comparison with others is one of the primary ways people continue to create more shame for themselves. The messages you heard growing up are the messages you continue to give yourself. You no longer need others to tell you to do better or what you do is not good enough. You do that fine by yourself. Since your efforts were never experienced as sufficient, adequate, or good enough, you did not develop an internal sense of just how much is good enough. As a consequence, there is always a hole in your gut, an emptiness, a sense of incompleteness. And for some, ultimately, a hopelessness.

I developed a perfectionist mind-set; anything short of being number one meant failure.

Procrastination

Perfectionism and procrastination are closely linked and people often identify with engaging in both. Procrastination, such as starting but not completing a project or considering a project but never initiating it, is often an attempt to defend against further shame. Some people procrastinate because in the desire to do things perfectly recognize it will never be good enough or their efforts won't be acceptable, so they stop or find safety in not trying.

For others, they received so little attention that they were not encouraged to initiate projects, let alone complete them. Too many times when they did something, drew a picture or wrote a story, and gleefully showed their mother or father, their parents barely looked at it and then set it aside or maybe even lost it. Without positive reinforcement to complete school projects or homework, children perform with ambivalence. They believe no one else cares and develop the attitude "Why should I care?" The result is procrastination.

It is possible you were humiliated for your efforts, made to feel inadequate or stupid. When that happens you find ways to protect yourself so you cease involvement in any action that would prove you really are a failure. In addition, you become discouraged when constantly compared to someone who did or might have done it better.

> *My two older brothers did well in school. They were quick to think on their feet and they were articulate. It took me longer to grasp things. I wasn't as interested in math and sciences as they were. I was more interested in my friends. So, with school being more of a struggle and having no real help from my parents, only the push that "you should be like your brothers," I just gave up. I wasn't like them and didn't want to be. So I just quit trying. I wasn't going to do it good enough anyway.*

Also mixed into procrastination may be anger, expressed as an attitude of "I'll show you—I won't finish this" or "I'll only do it part way. I won't give my best." Inherent in this attitude is a challenge that screams, "Like me for who I am, not for what I do." In a family where rigidity is the rule, where it is not okay to make mistakes, or to not be acknowledged for accomplishments or to have them demeaned, children learn not to initiate or finish what was started. For those raised this way, it is amazing anything gets completed.

> *If I did something wrong while I was driving, my father would backhand me in the mouth. Needless to say, it wasn't easy to drive with tears, frustration, and anger. I had four learner's permits by the time I was eighteen. I was twenty-two before I had enough courage to get my license, and I was twenty-seven before I could*

drive on the freeway. I still get scared today to try new things. I put them off and in many cases I simply don't try.

Victimization

I knew nothing about relationships. I didn't know what was appropriate to give in a relationship so I just gave, gave, and gave. I didn't know what my needs were. I didn't know how to ask for what I wanted. I didn't know what I wanted. I had learned no one really cared or was interested. My needs had never been met so I didn't expect that. So one relationship after the other, they were all alike. They took advantage of me; I have been slapped around a lot. I leave every relationship with less than I go in with.

People who succumb to the victim role do not know how to say no. They are struggling with the internalized beliefs of "I am not worthy," "I am not of value," "Other people are more important than me," or "Other people are more worthy," that will sabotage setting limits. They often have no boundaries or have distorted boundaries. The desperate longing for nurturance and care overrides the willingness to establish safe and appropriate boundaries with others.

Victims have learned not to trust their own perceptions, believing that another person's perceptions are more accurate than their own. They give others the benefit of the doubt and are willing to respond to the structure others set. Victims are skilled at adhering to the dysfunctional family rules. Victims operate from a position of fear, unable to access any anger or indignation that comes with being hurt, disappointed, or abused. When asked what they need or want, victims often literally do not know.

Almost inevitably, victims have great difficulty protecting themselves in the context of intimate relationships. They are often attracted to someone who appears to have the ability to take charge, make things happen. This is someone who very likely feels strengthened by association with the victim's vulnerability. Becoming highly skilled at rationalizing, minimizing, and, often, flatly denying the events and emotions in their lives, victims develop a high tolerance for pain and inappropriate behavior. To name hurtful or inappropriate behavior may be perceived as inviting more trouble in to their life. While the victim response is the result of the belief in personal powerlessness, it is also a defense. Victims believe they may not have as much pain if they give in and relinquish autonomy to someone else.

While some victims stay in isolation, those who don't often play a combination of the victim/martyr roles: "Look at how I am victimized. Aren't they terrible for doing this to me! I will just have to endure." Being the victim becomes part of a cycle. Victims already feel bad about themselves as a result of being abandoned and/or abused and don't act in a manner that could create safety and security leading to greater abandonment or abuse.

For all of the reasons noted above, whether male or female, the shameful person is at great risk of repeated victimization.

> *When I would hitchhike, guys would pick me up and not let me out until they got what they wanted. Then they would kick me out of the car and I'd put out my thumb again.*

Rage

Rage compensates for an overwhelming sense of powerlessness; it is the holding tank for accumulated fears, angers, humiliations, and shame. It is intended to protect against further experiences of pain. Emotionally, it is an attempt to be heard, seen, and valued when you are most desperate and lacking in other skills. When you have lived with a chronic sense of helplessness combined with fear, rageful behavior offers a sense of power. When rage is the only way people know to protect against emptiness, powerlessness, and pain, the choice is a quick one.

> *In my rage I don't feel inadequate or defective. It may be a false sense of power I feel, but if all I have ever known is my powerlessness, I'll take false power over no power.*

Rageful behavior also offers protection by keeping people at a distance. As a result, other people cannot see into the raging person's soul that he or she believes to be so ugly.

Many times people who are rageful grew up with parental rage. It was often the only model for attempting to be heard or to garner control. Rage as a defense also offers protection by transferring shame to others.

The outwardly rageful person chooses a victim-like person who, consciously or not, is willing to take the abuse or assume the shame. The rager chooses to live with people who become the chronic victim(s) of his or her rage; or move around a lot, wearing out his or her welcome after relatively short periods of time in one place.

> I had always looked outside for the answers. My life was such a mess and everything I did was just making it worse. I had been so lonely, so frightened. I had felt so empty and didn't know why; alcohol and rage were my answers. And I became addicted to the high of both.

Growing up some children find anger to be their one safe feeling. This leads to other vulnerable feelings being masked with anger. Many people full of rage show no sign of other emotions. They keep a tight lid on all of their feelings until something triggers an eruption and suddenly their rage is in someone else's face. Perhaps it is a scathing memo at work or an outburst of criticism toward a waiter or grocery store attendant. This is what I refer to as *machine gun bursts*.

The person who rages is often best described as holding a gas can in one hand and a lit match in the other.

While some people outwardly show chronic rage, others live with an internalized, simmering anger—a silent rage. When anger is held back and internalized, it grows. It festers into chronic bitterness or chronic depression. When there has been no outlet for anger, it is more apt to explode suddenly as a significant single hostile act.

Examples of this are the highly publicized acts of school violence and shootings across the country. The shooter is often described as having shown no previous signs of aggression. Much of the time the shooters were described as being loners or simply different, but not overtly violent.

After further investigation, however, it was discovered that these troubled individuals carried burdens of buried rage, often the result of being bullied within the family or by their peers in the schools that manifested in an act of deadly violence.

Rageful behavior is a combination of the inability to tolerate vulnerable feelings and the inability to resolve conflict and/or perceive options and choices. These dynamics are common consequences to growing up with addiction.

While my mom was the one addicted to alcohol and drugs, my dad was addicted to his rage. He would fly off the handle at anything and everything. He would rant and rave and kill you with his words. He actually looked like he enjoyed it. The scenes were right out of a movie. Only they were very real for us. I swore I wouldn't end up like my dad, and yet that is exactly what I do today. I understand the high he got in his rage; I understand the power he felt. And it is destroying everything in my life.

Depression

For many, depression is a biochemical imbalance or disordered neurochemistry, best treated with antidepressants. It is commonly accepted among professionals that depression tends to run in families, suggesting there may be a physiological predisposition toward depression. But depression is also induced by external experiences. For a number of people, it is a consequence of a habitually pessimistic and disordered way of viewing the world. Living with addiction certainly makes one see the world in a negative and chaotic manner. Depression is also the consequence of loss and the inability to do the grief work necessary to bring completion to the feelings of sorrow. It can be referred to as *pathological grief*. It is also a traumatic stress response when your survival response is to freeze, your neuro system is in a chronic state of hypo-arousal that fuels depression.

A depressed person is typically pictured as one who sleeps excessively, is unable to eat, and is suicidal. While that picture represents the severe end of the depression continuum, many depressed adults are able to function daily and meet many of their responsibilities. After all, for the adult child it has been his or her survival mode. Remember, looking-good children are often those who maintain the appearance of doing just fine outside while dying slowly on the inside. Children in addictive homes develop the skill of compartmentalizing. As a child, you may have cried yourself to sleep at night or lashed out in anger or hidden in fear, but when you got to school you didn't tell anyone about your feelings or experiences. You present yourself to the world as "I am fine; life is fine; and nothing is amiss." You present a false self who may not have had the look of depression, while your true self—emotional and spiritual self—was experiencing great despair. This is practiced day in and day out, week after week, month after month, and year after year. It easily becomes a skill that becomes a defense. As a consequence, many adult children do not demonstrate blatant depression but are a part of the walking wounded, the *closeted depressed.*

To keep depression hidden, people avoid sharing with others on an intimate level or avoid spending time with friends who may recognize their true feelings and internal despair or emptiness. They rely on defenses of busyness and accomplishing tasks. They deliberately keep the focus on other things and other people. They appear very capable and put out an impenetrable force field that says, "Don't ask me about myself. Don't push me."

It is difficult enough being depressed. It is even more difficult when you have shame around it—shame that fuels depression and more shame because you are depressed.

There is tremendous loss associated with being raised in a shame-based family. With the family being denial-centered, as it often is, and it not being okay to talk honestly, the sense of loss is amplified because there is no way to work through the pain. The hurt, the disappointment, the fears, and the anger associated with life events are all swirled together and internalized. Add to this a personal belief that says, "I am at fault" or "I am not worthy," then it is easy to see why you come to believe in your unworthiness and try to hide your real self from others. Eventually, you hit an emotional wall. The burden of hiding eventually becomes too heavy and all of those protecting, controlling mechanisms that kept your depression closeted just stop working. The ability to compartmentalize becomes so diminished and you are no longer able to hide the depression. By the time many adult children show obvious (overt) depression, it is usually little more than the final eruption of a long-term, chronic, closeted, hidden depression.

I didn't even know I was depressed until I was no longer depressed. I had always lived like this. I functioned. I operated in the world. I had a good job, family. But I have never felt joy. Oh, I am very socially skilled; no one knew how I felt over the years. Then one day, I just couldn't keep the pretenses up. None of my old defenses kept working. It was like I hit a wall I did not see coming.

Anxiety

A generalized anxiety disorder is marked by unrealistic worry, apprehension, and uncertainty. Think about that as a child growing up with addiction. There is so much uncertainty, unpredictability. Of course you would be apprehensive and, as a consequence, hypervigilant and worry about every possibility. As an adult that constant state of worry, apprehension, and hypervigilance has now become an habitual way of protection and survival. It may be unrealistic, but it is also a trauma response.

Courtney was raised in a physically abusive, alcoholic family. Between the ages of seven and twelve, she was also sexually abused by her older brother. At the age of thirty-six, she is self-supporting but lives her life quite isolated. She is hypervigilant to the first sign of danger, physical and emotional. She perceives danger when she feels misunderstood, not agreed with—limiting her social world considerably. She has been in the same job fifteen years, not wanting any advancement or change, liking the security. She is far too frightened of intimacy to allow herself a close and loving relationship. She lies awake at night, listening to noises, or frequently wakes up in the night, startled and unsure of her safety. From the outside, she simply looks like someone more introverted and content to live her life this way. All the while, she is simply trying to contain her fears. Courtney is struggling with anxiety that is a part of her post-traumatic stress.

As Courtney has done, most adult children accept their anxiety as a way of life, using their skills in denial and rationalizing as they live their daily lives.

Self-Harm

Those who struggle with depression and anxiety as a result of trauma often engage in physical acts of self-injury. The most common acts are cutting and burning, but self-harm can take many forms such as incessant pinching of skin or head-banging. While it makes no sense to the thinking brain that to escape from persistent pain you would create more physical pain, the act of self-harm often generates a dissociative response or a feeling of release and relief in the moment. It's an attempt to regulate the painful emotions of anger, sadness, anxiety, and shame.

Sleep Disturbances

Many adult children report they have difficulty sleeping with nightmares being common. They are hypervigilant to noises, feeling the need to be prepared to protect themselves and to respond to the threats that seem to always be lurking. Never having established a sense of emotional safety, the past plagues them. Substances are a common solution to nightmares, sleep disturbances, and internalized shame. For many, sleep time is the most challenging time.

Physical Illness and Chronic Pain

Traumatic stress contributes to digestive and autoimmune problems; it contributes to diabetes, heart disease, and various cancers. When the body is repeatedly plunged past its normal limits, it begins to break down. Long-term trauma responses can tax the body and create inflammation, compromising the immune system that in turn makes the body more vulnerable to illness. The Adverse Childhood Experiences Study (see

Appendix) that has been ongoing for over twenty years alarmingly shows a direct relationship between primary diseases and trauma. Experts in treating chronic pain see a direct relationship between trauma and physical pain in that the unhealed emotional trauma exacerbates the sensation of pain. The strong emotions of terror, sadness, grief, and shame become embedded in the body. There are several theories as to why this is so with evidence pointing to the chronically heightened stress response due to trauma occurring in the same parts of the brain that register pain.

Co-occurring Disorders of Depression, Anxiety, and Addiction

Depression and anxiety are frequently masked with addictive disorders.

Janet, raised with a single-parent drug-addicted mom, was ultimately treated for both depression and anxiety after her second divorce from two long-term marriages to addicts. Until the divorce, she had not reached out for help and by the time she sought it she was experiencing a major depression. She was experiencing slurred speech, the inability to make decisions, extremely poor self-care, diminished expectations, etc. The depression was treated with antidepressants. What then became obvious was a long-standing anxiety disorder. She fretted and worried about every minor and major detail in her life. Everything in life was a potential problem. To ask basic questions of someone in a store would send her into an emotional panic. Multiple times she was taken to the emergency room thinking she was having a heart attack to be diagnosed with a panic attack. What would not be identified because the mental health issues were more blatant and those doing the assessment did not include an addiction assessment, was that she had been addicted to pills for many years.

Ryan started experiencing panic attacks shortly after he began recovery from his compulsive overeating. He was raised in an alcoholic family with a schizophrenic mother who subjected him to extremely cruel physical punishments. Food had always been his medicator. Without the sugar and without any recovery from the emotional pain in his life, his fears quickly rose to the surface and he was hospitalized three times for what would ultimately be diagnosed as panic attacks characterized by intense anxiety, often a feeling of impending death, heart palpitations, shortness of breath, and sweating. Having been the victim of physical or sexual abuse strongly contributes to the likelihood of experiencing post-traumatic stress disorder.

Brad, thirty-six, had seen two family members die from their addictions yet here he was sitting at home in seclusion, with curtains drawn, drinking himself into oblivion. He was beginning to miss work on a regular basis. Fearful he would lose his job, he sought help. Three years sober, he found himself one more time, at home in seclusion, with curtains pulled. Although he was not drinking, he was in absolute despair. Once more, Brad would reach out for help. This time he would be treated for depression—depression that was present prior to getting sober but was not recognized. It was a depression strongly fueled from growing up with a lot of trauma in an addictive family.

Substances are seen as an answer to those who are depressed and anxious. Some people are looking to be numb, others are using to get a rush, to experience something different and greater than what they feel. Addiction to behaviors are common as well. Substances and processes both have satiating and arousal behaviors. Certain acts of gambling are more sedating, such as slot machines; others more arousing, such as horse racing or day trading. Some sexual behaviors are sedating and calming while others involve the arousal of risk. High intensity sports, contact sports, or the applause of an audience only elevate one's emotional state. Forms of escape or excitement are quick answers to a complex problem— the trauma of growing up with addiction.

When I gamble I feel a rush. I feel I hold the world in my hand. My concentration is so focused, every past, present, or future problem is obliterated from my reality!

I was engaged in compulsive masturbation by the time I was ten. As my parents kept me awake with their arguing late into the night, I found solace, peace, in self-touch alone in my bedroom. I began to drink beer, whiskey, anything I could find about age thirteen to medicate the shame I was feeling around my sexual behavior. Then I found if I drank enough, I felt this courage to approach girls sexually. As I got a bit older, then I discovered that if I used amphetamines I could go for hours sexually, then I'd use the alcohol to keep me from thinking about what I was doing. I am an addiction binger and trader. In time, it wasn't just sex, alcohol, drugs, I would satisfy my craving needs through food, work, anything, to try to feel normal.

Thoughts of Death

I am hopeless. I am unworthy. And I don't deserve to live.

If you live with enough fear, enough shame, and enough hopelessness, it only makes sense that at some point you begin to consider that maybe it would be better to not feel at all. It's so difficult to let people know that your despair and self-loathing takes you to that darkness, to that place of thinking you would be better off not being here at all. This thinking is far more common than not. This isn't a blatant suicidal thought; it is a thought though that can ultimately lead to finding solace in the concept of death. If you experience that thought frequently, the concept of death can become a comforting friend. The point being, people who grow up with trauma are certainly more apt to make a suicide attempt because they already have a friend in the thought of death. Suicidal thoughts and attempts are often a reflection of anger, rage turned inward, or the result of major depression. For some people, the attempt and act of suicide compensates for the powerlessness in their life. For most, death is perceived as a better option than living with certain memories and shame. The pain is too overwhelming. Out of despair and hopelessness, people become their own victims.

Life won't get any better, and I can't stand this pain.

If you find yourself thinking about the comfort of no longer being here or thinking about suicide, speak up and let someone know how frightened, angry, or hopeless you are feeling.

Repeating the Patterns

Whether or not the words *it will never happen to me* were ever spoken or just assumed, people raised in an addicted family system, despite all their good intentions, experience unhealed trauma and are more likely to repeat the familial patterns.

Addictive Disorders

If your great-grandfather, your grandfather, and your father had red hair, there is a strong probability that you have red hair and some of your children will, too. Addictive disorders and their many ramifications are similar. They, too, can pass from generation to generation. Though not all addicts learn their drinking and using behavior at their parents' knees, children frequently imitate the styles of their parents. When you come from a pain-based family, you frequently go outside of yourself for a quick answer to relieve your suffering. You need someone or something to relieve this intolerable pain, take away your profound loneliness, fear, and shame, so you seek a mood-altering experience. You need to escape. When you grow up in an environment where the cause of pain is external, you develop the belief that the solutions to problems exist only through substances or behaviors.

> *I can remember my first drink. I was eleven. I hated the taste, but I felt the glow and it worked. I would get sick as a dog and then swear on a stack of Bibles I would not do it again, but I kept going back. I got drunk because I had a hole in my gut so big, and alcohol and then other drugs would fill the hole. They became the solution.*

Whatever one's drug of choice, it can quickly become an anesthetizer. It is most likely the one modeled and most accessible. So if you grow up with a substance-use-disordered parent, it is often substances; if you grow up under the influence of a gambler, it is gambling; if you grow up in a family with sex addiction, you find yourself a sex addict as well. Or not. Possibly because you are so driven to make sure it will never happen to you, you seek out a different substance than your addicted parent. If dad was addicted to alcohol, you don't touch it, but you love your marijuana, you love your prescription pain pills, your meth. You don't recognize an addiction is an addiction but from the brain's viewpoint, substance and process addictions are identical.

Addiction is about the continued practice of an activity or the continued use of a substance despite negative consequences that ultimately interfere with portions of your life. Both substances and/or process addictions stimulate and reward the same neural pathways in the brain. Dopamine and adrenaline trigger the brain's pleasure reward center; serotonin lessens anxiety and depression; endorphins do both and reduce pain as well. These neurochemicals have another attribute—they increase your ability to later recall how great you felt. This encourages you to repeat the same experience again, again, and again. Addiction is not so much about a specific substance or activity as it is about disrupting the normal procession of pleasure and process of thinking. The part of the brain that allows you to think rationally, see choices and consequences, when under the influence, becomes hijacked leaving the brain to not consider consequences.

With the exception of some illicit drugs, these substances are an integral part of our culture, socially sanctioned and supported, making it very difficult for the abuser to initially recognize he or she is using them in unhealthy ways. In addition to temporarily controlling the emotional pain, the substances used and abused very often provide something one does not know how to seek naturally. They offer an illusion of power to someone who has known only powerlessness; courage and confidence to someone who feels lacking in both. This is certainly drug-induced, temporary, and false, but for many people, false courage, confidence, and power is better than no courage, no confidence, and no power. For someone who is isolated and feels alienated, the addictive behavior or substance may make it easier to reach out to people and not feel so alone. "Give me a little bit to drink and I become alive. I pull myself away from the wall and I find myself talking, laughing, and listening. I see people responding to me and I like it." This doesn't mean that a person is addicted, but it does mean he or she is thirsty for connection with others. And to maintain that connection or that sense of power or courage, is a set up to want a second, third, and fourth drink, toke, snort, or whatever in order to feel more calm, whole, and complete.

People who have never taken time to play or laugh because life has been so serious find alcohol gives them the opportunity to relax. Anne identified, "My entire life has been spent taking care of other people. I am always busy. I make these lists daily, thinking the world will stop if I don't get the job done. I don't think about missing out on fun—it has never been a part of my life. I never drank until I was twenty-six. I don't even know why I started. Those first few times I heard myself laugh with other people it actually scared me. I remember thinking that I was being silly as if that was bad. Yet at the same time there was this attraction. It was as if there was this whole other part of me I didn't know and maybe was okay to know. The attraction to relaxing with alcohol kept getting stronger. I can actually remember thinking, I don't have to make this decision tonight or I don't have to do this by myself. Pretty soon, it was I don't have to do this at all. I was having fun. Life wasn't so hard."

Because Anne did not know how to relax, she was tightly controlled in her thoughts and emotions and she ultimately became dependent. She, like so many others, was seeking wholeness. But the only glimpse she had of feeling whole, feeling complete was under the influence.

Addictive behaviors, whether they are substances or processes, provide something the adult child has not learned to acquire naturally, such as courage, confidence, laughter, power, or connections to others. Common process addictions range from compulsive activities, such as gambling, gaming, spending, sexual behaviors, disordered eating behaviors, relationship dependencies, work addiction, and compulsive busyness. People use any and all of these to distance or distract, to get their mind off their pain. Many behavioral compulsions would be otherwise harmless activities if they weren't exaggerated, destroying the balance in your life. For example, exercise is a healthy activity until done so excessively that you injure yourself. Addiction is about living in the extreme without a sense of moderation.

By fourth grade I was preoccupied with food. I told myself in a proud way that I was addicted to Coca-Cola, just like Mom was addicted to booze.

Spending and shopping give me a sense of power. For just a little while it can feel so great.

There was so much pain I was forever seeking ways to escape. As a child it was food, fantasy reading, and television. I was always looking for someplace safe. I never felt safe. I never felt good about myself or even adequate. I was never enough. My sex addiction is about paying for women who will not reject me. They are safe. I get consumed with the ritual of finding them; it's me in a fantasy world again. All the pressures I feel, the anxiety that for me comes with living, are gone. Then I go back to my guilt and shame, and then cycle back to the hunt.

As with addictions, abuses repeat themselves within families as well.

Dad was a great teacher and I was his prize pupil. I picked up all of his self-centeredness, dishonesty, demanding, false promises, his addiction, and his outright abusive behavior, plus all of the guilt, remorse, and low self-esteem that goes with it. I had always sworn I'd never be like Dad—but ultimately I got there.

While not all abusers learn their behavior in their parents' home, the overwhelming tendency is to punish as you were punished, to resolve conflict the way you saw it resolved, to construct your relationships as your parents did, and to continue to tolerate the levels of abuse you witnessed in childhood.

Just as you comment to yourself or others *it will never happen to me*, convinced you will not become addicted or ever marry someone who is addicted, the adult child does that with violence as well. Anger burns out of control in abusive families. As a result, the child is usually someone who becomes anger-avoidant, terrified of any anger, his or others, or he, too, becomes abusive in his anger. Children of anger frequently marry or are in committed relationships with someone who is chronically angry or rageful, or abusive in his or her own anger.

I was so afraid of any conflict, any anger, I'd do anything to placate, to please my husband, but in reality that did very little to stop his rage.

> *I would have private temper tantrums. I'd throw things, slam doors, and swear a lot. I'd become enraged at the slightest frustration—getting stuck in traffic or losing my keys and not being able to get the door open. All the things I'd locked in as a child were slowly slipping out.*

> *I was a strict disciplinarian. I would spank and then lose control. I always responded to whatever my kids did in a physical way. Afterward, I would be so appalled by what I had done. Even more so, I was appalled I was just like my father. I felt mortified with shame. But I couldn't seem to stop myself, and the beatings continued.*

Self-hate is overwhelming for the person raised with violence. Low self-esteem, coupled with a pervasive sense of powerlessness and fear of conflict, often compels someone to choose a partner who also has low self-esteem and acts out his or her low self-worth in a similar manner. The person raised with violence has internalized the words and behaviors that repetitively said she was worthless; she was not deserving; she would never amount to anything; or she couldn't do anything right. Such individuals frequently succumb to depression, believing in their helplessness and hopelessness. Others resort to addictive behaviors. Many become abusers.

Alicia was sexually abused by her father, her brothers, and then her brother's friends. She was having sex with any guy she knew by the time she was a teenager. "I was fourteen and all I knew about myself was I could do two things well. One was to drink and the other was to get a guy to bed. They were my points of pride."

Often sex is the only way one knows to get attention because it is basically the only way he or she was ever given attention. Alicia's only validation for being was through being sexual and, ultimately, she found her only power through sex. Promiscuity is a misguided search for love, nurturing, and acceptance, but it does not work. Alicia went to treatment for drug abuse when she was twenty-three, but she would also be treated for sex addiction and the underlying trauma of being sexually abused.

It is easy to be involved in sexually abusive relationships when one's sexual boundaries have been repeatedly violated. As the survivor feels dirty and doesn't know how to say no, more shame is incorporated, greater helplessness is experienced, and then more repetition occurs.

Josh, raised by two substance-abusing parents, experienced more covert sexual abuse by his father and more blatant abuse by his mother. His father wouldn't allow the boys to wear nightclothes, and then he would wander the house nude and drunk. He teased the boys mercilessly about their sexual development. His dad often drank outside of the home, leaving Josh home alone with his mother where she did her drinking. The older brothers were often out on the streets. "I needed love and attention from my mom, but then she'd go into this striptease and molest me. I wanted her to stop, but I didn't know how. I felt so powerless. I thought I should have known what to do, how to get myself out of this situation. I should have been a grown-up and done the right thing. I had this terrible sense of shame because I didn't know what to do. I didn't know how to get away from my pain." Josh started making suicide attempts beginning at the age of nine, and began drinking and using Valium by age twelve. He moved into his sex addiction in his later teens and began to sexually abuse and traffic young girls.

The combination of the physical act of being victimized, improper role modeling accompanied by feelings of fear, guilt, anger, and shame leads to various fight, flight, and freeze responses for the child. Addiction for so many is the fight and the flight.

Repetition in Relationships

As surprising as it is for the person involved, it is as common for children raised with addiction to marry or to enter into committed relationships (and often times more than once) with someone with an addiction as it is for them to become addicted to a substance or behavior. And it is just as common if they experienced physical or sexual abuse for that to occur in the context of their new family as well.

Dynamics that create the likelihood of repetition:

- The stage of progression is significant particularly for people in their first adult relationship. When both you and this partner are younger, you are more likely to have met when he or she is in the earlier stages rather than middle or late stages of the addictive disorder. Many adult children are less likely to have any memory of their addicted parent's early stage behavior. By the time you are old enough for memory, your parent is into the middle or even later stages of his or her addiction. It is very difficult to identify addiction in the earlier stages, as the behaviors are so inconsistent.

- The person you partner with may be addicted to a different substance or behavior than the one you were raised with so you don't see the blatant similarities. To assure yourself you don't marry someone like your parent, for example, someone who is alcoholic, you marry someone who drinks very little or not at all. But, lo and behold, he or she ends up being addicted to cocaine or another drug, or they have a process addiction, such as gambling, porn addiction, or another addictive process.
- You recognize your partner has a problem, but you tell yourself you can handle it. You believe you have the advantage of knowing what to expect. After all, you have handled your parent's problem and you tell yourself you can handle this as well telling yourself it won't be that bad. You loved your mother or father in spite of his or her addiction, and you will love this person in spite of his or her addiction.
- Adult children often have what is called *impoverished expectations*—you don't expect enough. This is usually based in low self-esteem, not believing you deserve differently or better. It is also based in having had years of minimizing, denying, and pretending things are other than they are. That doesn't change just because you are older.
- Another adult-child trait is a high tolerance for inappropriate behavior that allows the addictive behavior to not be recognized for what it is, and to minimize the pain and disruption it causes you or the relationship.

These multiple factors make it very easy to repeat a family pattern.

As I was growing up, I remember really wanting only one thing—to be able to do it differently than I saw it being done around me. So, when, two days before my twenty-third birthday, my husband was put in jail for a felony DUI, I looked into the passive eyes of my child, whom I had just thrown across the room, and felt my world and my sanity crumble. I was doing it just the same way they had done.

Due to the dynamics of growing up with addiction, relationships in general can be problematic. The modeling you had was controlling, abusive, apathetic, noncommittal, acrimonious, and, often, addictive. Leaving you to engage in similar, controlling, abusive, apathetic, noncommittal, acrimonious, and addictive behaviors. You believe your worth and value only exists within the context of a coupleship. Relationship dependency is fueled by low self-esteem and lack of a strong sense of self. The adult child uses the relationship as proof of worthiness. In an addictive relationship you use other people to lessen your shame and to avoid facing yourself. To be outside of a relationship is too frightening. To be alone often puts you in touch with your emptiness. Being in a relationship allows you to focus on others without having to address your own pain. The problem with this is it's a set up to tolerate hurtful behavior, to not be assertive, and to not grow. At the price of your own well well-being, the adult child will go to any lengths to maintain or get into a relationship.

Signs of relationship and love addiction:

- Confusing love with intensity and/or frequency of sex.
- Being with a partner who is unavailable or highly controlling.
- Compromising values in order to secure or keep a relationship.
- Lacking boundaries, not being able to say no when you want to.
- Intimacy is based in fantasy and magical thinking.
- Living in fear the relationship could end at any time, after all, you believe you are not good enough.
- Engaging in high-risk sexual behaviors; the risk-taking often out of fear of losing the relationship.
- Rushing into another relationship prematurely, often having a potential partner waiting in the wings.

Shelly captures the core of relationship and love addiction, "I have been married and divorced five times, and now I realize I never divorced the right man all along, my father."

CHAPTER SEVEN

The Adult Child Begins Recovery

Children raised with addiction move into adulthood with incredible strengths as a result of survivorship. They pat themselves on the back and don't want to look behind at the past, but in time they begin to experience problems as a result of:

- The inability —to trust their own perception.
  —to trust others.
  —to identify needs.
  —to identify feelings.
  —to listen.
  —to relax.
  —to initiate.
- Fear —of feelings.
  —of conflict.
  —of rejection or abandonment.
- The need to control.
- Impoverished expectations.
- Unrealistic expectations.
- High tolerance for inappropriate behavior.
- Approval seekers.
- Rage.

- Depression.
- Substance use disorders.
- Process addictions.
- Disordered eating.
- Repetitive addictive relationships.

To some degree we can all be affected by these issues. But the phrase "some degree" is important here. Adult children experience these difficulties to an extreme; difficulties that can interfere with the ability to genuinely discover happiness and meaningfulness in life. It is my belief that adult children deserve more than the ability to survive.

Recovery begins with accepting two basic rights:

1. The right to talk about the real issues.
2. The right to feel.

Steps in Recovery

Judith Viorst wrote in *Necessary Losses,* "It is true that as long as we live we may keep repeating the patterns established in childhood. It is true that the present is powerfully shaped by the past. But it is also true that insight at any age keeps us from singing the same sad songs again."

To be able to put the past behind and not repeat those same sad songs, adult children need to take the following steps.

- **Explore Past History**

  You need to explore your past, your childhood years, to discover and acknowledge your reality, not to assign blame. It is my belief that family members truly want the best for each other and that begins with self-honesty. You aren't betraying your parents or siblings when you become honest about your reality. If there is an act of betrayal, it is with the addiction, the dysfunction of the family system. When you do not talk honestly about your experiences you ultimately betray yourself.

  Exploring past history means asking questions such as "What happened that was hurtful to me?" and "What didn't I have that I needed?"

To let go of the past you must be willing to break through denial to be able to grieve the pain. In other words, you need admit to yourself the truth of what happened, rather than hide or keep secret the hurt and wounds that occurred. It is difficult to speak honestly today when you have had to deny, minimize, or discount the first fifteen or twenty years of your life. There is no doubt denial became a skill that served you as a child in a survival mode. Unfortunately, denial, which begins as a defense, becomes a skill that interferes with how you live your life today. You take the skill of minimizing, rationalizing, and discounting into every aspect of your life. When you let go of denial and acknowledge the past, it gives you the opportunity to identify your losses and to grieve the pain associated with those losses. It is the opportunity to genuinely put the past behind. Exploring the past is an act of empowerment.

In the process of exploring your past, you are also doing grief work. Grieving that which you never had, grieving the losses that occurred. This takes you into the second step.

- **Moving into Your Emotions**

These steps are not linear, these two steps in particular are extremely entwined. Talking honestly about the past remains an intellectual exercise if the feelings that accompany the experiences are not acknowledged and felt. Because it is emotional and trusting yourself with feelings is not necessarily the strong suit of most adult children, it is important to have a safety net in place. When you have a history of cutting yourself off from feelings and they begin to rise, it often feels like a tsunami of all kinds of feelings. You need to know and to trust a support system.

Feelings have often been experienced as something to dread, to be afraid of. To be willing to embrace them, it is helpful to recognize the gifts they offer. For example, anger often leads to energy for those who have been immobilized or frozen and if used well leads to assertiveness; fear links to a gift of alertness and preservation; guilt allows people to make amends and helps keep them in touch with their values; with joy one can access gratitude. All feelings when listened to are cues and signals that tell you what

you need. "I'm scared and confused . . . I need . . ." "I am sad . . .
I need . . ." For the adult child who struggles with knowing his
or her needs, it begins with knowing his or her feelings. Feelings
don't necessary indicate action is needed as much as they need to
be heard and listened to. You are the first to do that with yourself.
Keep in mind that exploring your feelings is far more important
than accessing particular memories.

As noted this is only one step in the healing process. If it is
the only step you take it becomes a blaming process not a grief
process. Blaming parents has never been the intent of adult-child
recovery nor should it be. In your recovery you need a venue, be it
with a therapist, support group, or a workbook where you need to
say things such as "It wasn't fair." "They were wrong." " They hurt
me." This is a part of owning the experience. So much of what has
occurred was wrong and it hurt. Today you have lived with the
consequences. As you move through recovery you now need to be
accountable for the choices you make around your own healing.

- **Connect the Past to the Present**
  The purpose for connecting the past to the present is because the
  present is that which is most important. You cannot do anything
  about the past, but since your current life is so strongly influenced
  by your childhood experience, it is essential to take these steps so
  that you can reflect and grieve those aspects of your past. That
  being said, it is your life today that you want to fulfill. Connect
  the past to the present means asking, "How does this past pain
  and trauma influence who I am today? How does the past affect
  who I am as a parent, in the workplace, in a relationship, how I
  feel about myself?" The cause-and-effect connections you discover
  between past losses and present life will give you direction. These
  questions allow you to become more centered in the here and now.
  This clarity will identify the areas to focus on in recovery.

- **Challenge Core Beliefs**
  Challenge core beliefs means asking, "What beliefs have I
  internalized from my growing-up years? Are they helpful or hurtful
  to me today? What beliefs would support me in living a healthier

life?" Adult children often internalize beliefs such as "It is not okay to say no" or "Other people's needs are more important than my own" or "No one will listen to what I have to say" or "The world owes me and I am entitled" or "People will take advantage of me every chance they can." Many of the beliefs adult children have internalized are shame-based. "Who I am is not okay." "I am not worth anything." "I am defective, damaged." On the other hand, you may have internalized beliefs that said, "There are people who care," "I have value," "I deserve to live my life differently," etc. An important part of recovery is identifying, challenging, and letting go of specific beliefs that fuel self-defeating behaviors and low moods and recreating new beliefs that support you in the way you deserve to live. It is also recognizing childhood beliefs that supported you in a healthy way and continuing to embrace them. Today you can take ownership for maintaining those beliefs.

- **Grounding Practices**
  It will be difficult to do the above steps without engaging in grounding practices, which are ways to help you stay emotionally stable versus reactive or numb. These are tools that assist you in emotional regulation to not move into fight, flight, or freeze responses. To heal you need some inner stability, and you garner that when you have healthy ways in which to soothe yourself and feel safe in your own skin. Grounding practices are essential in every step of healing. They are not meant to be used a few times but throughout your entire recovery process. The good news is they are readily available and many of you may find you have already naturally gravitated toward them. That could account for some of the resiliency you are already demonstrating.
  Some common forms of grounding include:
    - Arts, such as painting, pottery, sculpting, photography.
    - Crafts, such as beadwork, needlepoint, woodworking, quilting, knitting.
    - Dancing.
    - Singing.
    - Time in nature.

- Time with animals.
- Gardening.
- Engagement in martial arts.
- Tai Chi.
- Yoga.
- Meditation practices.

As said, these practices are not meant to be used once or twice, Ideally, they are regular practices you integrate into your life. They calm racing thoughts, improve your ability to concentrate, increase energy, reduce anxiety, lessen depression, reduce emotional reactivity, inspire creativity, and increase compassion for yourself and others. They can be fun and can offer meaning in your life.

- **Learn New Skills**
All children of addiction learned important skills that are helpful to them. Reflect on the skills you learned that were helpful. Some learned to problem-solve, to take charge and lead, others established goals, some became good listeners, and others developed specific talents such as cooking. But what were the skills you did not learn? You may not have learned to ask for help, to set limits for yourself, to express feelings in a healthy way, or to relax. Reviewing the progression of the roles in Chapter Four will help you identify some of those skills. The question you need to ask yourself is "What did I not learn that would help me today?" Many skills were learned prematurely and were developed from a basis of fear and shame. When that occurs there is a tendency to feel like an imposter and in those situations, addressing the feelings and beliefs associated with the skill will make it more likely you can feel greater confidence in those skills. You were resilient and those skills you get to keep.

This step and the next are the two that are most linear of all of them. This means the previous steps need to be taken before you act on these. The reason for that is the skills you may want to learn that you didn't get to learn as a child have both an emotional component and a belief system attached to them. And those feelings are often painful and the belief system often self-defeating due to it emanating from a traumatic childhood. For example, a good behaviorist can help you learn the skill of limit-setting, role-play situations in which you demonstrate the skill. Yet in real life, when you go to practice, you hit a wall if you did not address the emotions and beliefs that many years ago were attached to the experiences that made it unsafe for you to learn this skill. It is possible you couldn't set limits because you came to believe you didn't have the right to protect yourself or that when you set limits others wouldn't like you. Those are beliefs that continue to get in the way of the skill if you don't identify and challenge them and create new ones in their place. In addition, the emotional pain you felt at those times in childhood when you wanted to set limits for yourself but couldn't and, therefore, often felt sad, embarrassed, or afraid, still need to be acknowledged. To learn new skills requires feeling safe within yourself to acknowledge feelings and to identify the beliefs that could sabotage the new skill.

The change you want to create in your life will be made directly as a result of undoing your denial process and grieving the pain. It means recognizing the connection of the past to present day. It necessitates owning the beliefs you want to carry and letting go of old, hurtful belief systems and learning skills that were never modeled or the opportunity never afforded. With the incorporation of grounding practices into these steps it becomes possible to create a **new narrative** for yourself. These steps walk you through owning a narrative of your past, a past strongly impacted by addiction. Now you have the opportunity to create and live a new, more positive narrative that comes with the tools of your recovery and healing.

You no longer have to live with the script of the past but have choices as to how you live your life.

The following exercises are a start to your self-exploration.

Breaking the Don't Talk Rule

One of the consequences of growing up in a home with the Don't Talk rule is that people develop a silent tolerance for inconsistencies, untruths, and painful feelings. Reflect on people you may have talked to about problems at home when you were a young child and teenager. Check the frequency with which you can remember talking about problems to your:

	Never	Once	Occasionally	Often
Mother	☐	☐	☐	☐
Father	☐	☐	☐	☐
Stepmother	☐	☐	☐	☐
Stepfather	☐	☐	☐	☐
Brother	☐	☐	☐	☐
Brother	☐	☐	☐	☐
Sister	☐	☐	☐	☐
Sister	☐	☐	☐	☐
Grandparents	☐	☐	☐	☐
Other family members	☐	☐	☐	☐
Teacher	☐	☐	☐	☐
Counselor	☐	☐	☐	☐
Clergy	☐	☐	☐	☐
Friend	☐	☐	☐	☐
Neighbor	☐	☐	☐	☐
Other	☐	☐	☐	☐

In some instances, certain issues were present in your family life that may have prevented you from talking about problematic areas of your life. Circle those that were true for you:

I felt ashamed.

I felt disloyal, as if I were betraying.

I was embarrassed.

I didn't understand what was occurring well enough to talk about it.

I was afraid I wouldn't be believed.

I was specifically instructed not to talk.

It was insinuated in nonverbal ways that I should not talk.

It seemed as though no one else was talking.

I believed something bad would happen if I talked.

I came to believe that nothing good would have come from talking.

If as an adult, you still have difficulty talking about your growing-up years put a check (✓) by the above statement(s) that apply to you today.

List the people in your life today with whom you already are or are willing to talk to about your growing-up years:

1. _____

2. _____

3. _____

4. _____

5. _____

6. _____

7. _____

If you:

- Feel a sense of shame when talking about your growing-up years, try to understand that you weren't at fault—your parents would have liked it to have been different.
- Feel a sense of guilt, trust that you are not betraying your parents, your family, or yourself. If there is any betrayal, you are betraying the addictive system.
- Feel a sense of confusion about your childhood, that's probably an accurate description of how life has been for you—confusing. When attempting to explain irrational behavior in a rational manner, it will sound confusing. Talk—it will help you develop greater clarity.
- Fear that you will not be believed, a great deal of information is available that will substantiate that your experiences are not unique.
- Have been instructed, specifically or nonverbally, not to talk, recognize that instruction was motivated by fear or guilt. You don't have to live that way any longer.
- Have experienced something negative from people you spoke with in the past, you are now free to choose a healthier support system.
- Have been conditioned to believe that "nothing good comes from talking," put faith in the belief it is only when you finally begin to speak your truth that you will be able to put the past behind and experience the joy of the present.

Breaking the Don't Feel Rule

Painful feelings are more likely to lessen when you are able to talk about them. When you don't express these feelings they accumulate. As a scared young child, you began rolling your feelings up in a bundle like a small piece of snow rolling down a hill and now these feelings have become a giant snowball. By the time the snowball reaches the bottom of the hill— by the time you have grown up—the feelings have been piled up, painful upon painful feelings. No wonder you are scared. It's understandable that when you do get in touch with all your feelings, you may feel overwhelmed.

Present-day disappointments, losses, angers, and fears become intertwined with old disappointments, losses, angers, and fears, making it difficult to separate the old issues from the new ones. Having a feeling does not mean you need to act on it. How one feels and what one does with those feelings are separate issues. In early recovery, being aware of your feelings and identifying them are significant. Let your feelings be your friend, not something to be denied or minimized. Feelings are not there to rule you, but to be cues and signals to tell you something. Acceptance of feelings, combined with the ability to express them, will decrease fear and generate greater inner confidence. Feelings seem inappropriate only when they are not understood.

- What are the messages that interfere with your willingness to show specific feelings?
- Where did you get these messages?
- What is the price you pay for maintaining these messages?

If you are inexperienced at owning your feelings, it will be important for you to know the value of being able to identify and express them. Some benefits are:

- When I know my feelings and am more honest with myself, then I have the option of being more honest with others.
- When I am in touch with my feelings, I will be in a better position to be close to other people.
- When I know how I feel, I can begin to ask for what I need.
- When I am able to experience feelings, I feel more alive.

Identify two more reasons that are of value to be able to identify and express feelings.

Remind yourself of these messages by writing them down and posting them in a visible place or using them as affirmations to support you on a daily basis.

From the list below, circle the feelings with which you identify.

Love	Shame
Fear	Happiness
Worry	Guilt
Sadness	Confusion
Discouragement	Frustration
Anger	Loneliness
Hurt	Embarrassment
Jealousy	Hate

After you identify what you are feeling, note when and where you experience these feelings. If the identification of feelings is difficult, practice this on a daily basis. Try to share these with another person. The more specific you can be about your feelings, the more you can understand and accept them, and the more apt you are to be able to do something constructive with them. While positive feelings are the ones people seek, negative feelings can be viewed as cues or signals that can give information about what is needed.

When I feel sad, it may mean I need support.

When I am angry, I probably need to clarify my stance.

When I am scared, I need to let someone else know that.

By viewing the more painful feelings as signals, it is easier to accept them and to utilize them constructively. By identifying feelings, one is less apt to be overwhelmed by emotion and end up depressed, confused, or enraged.

With the following exercise you can gain insight into and awareness of family patterns. On a scale of one to five—one being the least often expressed, five being the most often expressed—rate your parents' frequency of expression.

FEELINGS	Mother	Father
Love	1 2 3 4 5	1 2 3 4 5
Fear	1 2 3 4 5	1 2 3 4 5
Worry	1 2 3 4 5	1 2 3 4 5
Sadness	1 2 3 4 5	1 2 3 4 5
Discouragement	1 2 3 4 5	1 2 3 4 5
Anger	1 2 3 4 5	1 2 3 4 5
Hurt	1 2 3 4 5	1 2 3 4 5
Jealousy	1 2 3 4 5	1 2 3 4 5
Shame	1 2 3 4 5	1 2 3 4 5
Happiness	1 2 3 4 5	1 2 3 4 5
Guilt	1 2 3 4 5	1 2 3 4 5
Confusion	1 2 3 4 5	1 2 3 4 5
Frustration	1 2 3 4 5	1 2 3 4 5
Loneliness	1 2 3 4 5	1 2 3 4 5
Embarrassment	1 2 3 4 5	1 2 3 4 5
Hate	1 2 3 4 5	1 2 3 4 5

You can also ask yourself which feelings you wanted expressed more often, and which ones less.

Can you see any repetitive patterns for you in adulthood?

Crying: The Expression of Sadness

As a child you may have learned not to cry or to cry silently alone. Thirty-six-year-old Anthony, a recovering addict, was talking about crying. He said he was the child who never cried. When he was very young, he remembered crying only once, and that was when a dog died. He entered adolescence and adulthood being "tough" and "surviving."

Anthony told his counselor about his complete inability to shed tears over any of his personal misfortunes, which included his nine hospitalizations for addiction. Surrender is essential for an addict's recovery. It includes the breaking of the denial system about one's situation in life, mentally, emotionally, physically, and spiritually. Anthony's surrender began when the tears started to flow the day he was admitted to his tenth treatment program. He needed to cry—he needed to quit being "tough," "alone," and in the denial trap of not talking, not feeling, and not trusting. The tears were the breakthrough. If you are an adult child who can identify with patterns of not crying or crying alone and silently, know your tears are not there to hurt you—they are there to cleanse your grief, your pain.

While many adult children struggle with the willingness to cry, there are those who find themselves frequently crying, yet not understanding the reason for the tears. Some find they cry at inappropriate times, while others find they cry at the appropriate times, but there is an overabundance of tears. They feel as if the depth of tears does not match the trigger. Cheryl, thirty-five, says, "I'm so tired of crying. I never cried as a child, and today I cry at the least little thing. I cry if I get scared; I cry if I feel rejected; I cry if I hear a sad story on the news; I cry when I read a nice, warm story on the internet. I don't seem to have any control. It's really embarrassing, but more than anything, it depletes me." In Cheryl's case, her crying incessantly has occurred in the first few months of her recovery process. The intensity and the frequency lessens when you are getting support at the same time. You have a lot to cry about and more likely than not it feels foreign. People describe feeling out of control, which is understandable when you have spent years working hard to hold in your pain. Holding the pain inside is what felt safe, sharing it, exposing it will feel foreign initially because it is unfamiliar to you. In time, you will feel relief. It is important to 1) recognize the need to cry; 2) give yourself permission; 3) let another person know about this; and 4) let that other person be available to offer support.

You will need to reevaluate the messages you previously received about crying, such as "It doesn't do any good to cry"; "Boys don't cry"; "Only sissies cry"; "I'll smack you harder if you cry." New messages need to be "It's okay if I cry"; "It's important that I allow myself to cry"; "It's a healthy release"; "I'll probably feel better."

As a child what did you do with your tears?

- Did you cry?
- Did others know when you were crying?
- Did you let others comfort you when you were crying?
- What did you do to prevent yourself from crying?

Now ask yourself:
- Do you ever cry?
- When do you cry?
- Do you only cry when alone?
- Do you cry hard, or do you cry slowly and silently?
- Do you cry because people hurt your feelings?
- Do you cry for no apparent reason?
- Do others know when you cry?
- Do you let others comfort you when you cry?
- What do you do to prevent yourself from crying?
- Do you get angry with yourself for crying?
- How is your pattern as an adult different from that of a child?

Read through these questions again, slowly, and then share what you know about yourself with another person. Choose a person with whom you feel safe—a therapist, a twelve-step member, a sponsor, a friend—someone with whom you feel you can allow yourself to be vulnerable. Remember, they may have old messages about the stigma of crying, too, and might welcome the opportunity to talk about an issue many people never take the time to explore.

You may also need to think about the basis of your fear. For the highly controlling person, fear of crying usually means a fear of falling apart. It is a fear of losing control; the fear that once crying starts, it will lead to hysterical behavior or that you will be unable to stop. The greater your fear, the greater the need to let others offer support. Recognize the need to establish a situation that is both protective and healthy. While crying may feel frightening, you do not need to fear you will go into hysteria. You may cry for five minutes, even ten minutes. As a therapist, I have seen hundreds of people cry, and they never needed to be carted away! Remember, you have accumulated a great deal of unresolved feelings. Your tears are usually related to sorrow, confusion, loneliness, and loss.

Fear

You may experience an overwhelming sense of fear. Much of the time that fear is unidentifiable. These fearful times are often episodic, periods of extreme fearfulness contrasted by periods totally devoid of fear. On the other hand, you may find yourself existing in a perpetual state of unidentifiable fear.

Many people are fearful of expressing their needs, fearing a loss of love should they express a want. Dawn said, "I've grown a lot, but I still feel gut-level fear when I express my wants and needs to my husband. It's difficult to be spontaneously open and self-disclosing. I'm afraid he won't love me." As you move from childhood to adulthood, you may continue to experience fear of confrontation. While most confrontation is a simple disagreement or questioning, as an adult child your experience was different. These fears persist because there was never any constructive or healthy disagreement within the family. Any expressed disagreement resulted in yelling and loud arguing because the parent could not tolerate anyone disagreeing with him or her. Disagreement was perceived as betrayal and resulted in actions that belittled and condemned the child.

When I think about my Dad drinking again I get shakey inside

I feel scared about things and worry most when everything is OK. I feel tied up and can't let go. I want to untie the knots and be free.

Janice, 44

Adult children who experienced a lot of fear of the unknown, never knowing what to expect next, will continue to experience uncertainty and fear of the unknown. The fear of the unknown can keep one immobilized, and being stuck in fear itself immobilizes one emotionally. It will result in a tendency to discount one's own perceptions and not have the courage to check out other people's perceptions. The results are isolation, low self-esteem, and, frequently, depression and anxiety.

Answer the following questions:

- What did you fear as a child?
- Did you fear you were going to be left alone?
- Were you afraid you were going to get hit?
- Were you afraid your mom or your dad did not love you?
- What did you do when you were fearful as a child?
- Did you go to your room and cry?
- Did you hide in a closet?
- Did you ask a brother or sister to come and be with you?
- Did you wet the bed?
- Did you mask your fear with anger?
- Did others know that you were afraid?
- Do you think your mom or dad knew?
- Do you think your grandparents knew?
- How is that pattern similar in your adulthood?
- Do you still go off by yourself when afraid?
- Do you still get angry instead?
- Are you sharing your fears with someone, or are you still pretending you're not afraid?

Ask those questions of another adult, someone you trust, and share your answers with one another. A goal in recovery is not to feel less than or be immobilized in fear. Fear can be a wonderful motivator and certainly a cue to what you may need.

Anger

The feeling of anger is natural to everyone, but when you are raised with addiction, anger is often repressed, twisted, and distorted. Adult children are usually either totally detached from, extremely frightened of, or overwhelmed by their anger. If you don't feel anger, ask yourself, "Where did it go? Why isn't it safe?" Be open to the fact that anger does exist. It is there. It just may not be very visible. When it was not safe for you to own your anger you take it elsewhere and it gets manifested in a multitude of ways—depressive behavior, overeating, oversleeping, placating, and illness, self-harm, addiction, psychosomatic problems. You may have experienced living with chronic anger or rage or an always-simmering low-level of anger or anger avoidance. Often one parent operates on one extreme, while the other parent is at the opposite extreme. Anger is often expressed through a tense silence, through mutual blaming, or through one-sided blaming coupled with one-sided acceptance. Typically in adulthood, the adult child repeats one of those extremes and most often chooses a mate to parallel that pattern.

Rich, age thirty-one, was aware of his anger but didn't find outlets for expression. "I have needed to let go of the bitterness and hatred. I see I have denied myself so much. I have not let myself get close to anybody, men or women. I have allowed myself to be eaten up inside. Oh, I looked okay to the world and have done okay in my work, but I can't let anyone get close enough to me or they would see this ugliness."

Jaclyn described the consequence to her fear of any conflict erupting into violence. "After four years of marriage in which there were very few arguments, I woke my husband one morning and said, I'm leaving now, and smiled." She said there had been no discussion of her wanting out of the marriage or her wanting anything to be different. She said she wasn't angry, she simply wanted out. She had never been allowed to disagree as a child and when her husband raised his voice, which she said wasn't too often, she'd simply agree to his wants. She walked out of a marriage that possibly could have been saved had she had the ability to simply disagree, had she had the ability to express what it was she needed or wanted. But for her, the fear of dealing with anger, either her own or her husband's, was too great to risk.

While some adult children are anger-avoidant and many others chronically angry or simply bitter about life, all have a definite need to resolve issues. While anger is a natural human emotion, what you do with anger is learned and can be reshaped to better meet your own needs. Remember, feelings are a natural part of you, use them as signals to help direct you.

Now ask yourself:

- What did you do with your anger as a child?
- Did you swallow and not become aware of it?
- Did you play the piano extra hard?
- If you played sports, were you more aggressive than you needed to be?
- Did you hit your brothers and sisters?
- Did you go to your room and cry?
- What did other family members do with their anger?
- Did your mom or dad just drink more?
- Did your brother just shrug his shoulders and go outside and play with his friends?
- Did your sister just cry silently?
- Are you afraid you will go into a rage?
- Is there a fear about what would happen if you really acknowledged your anger today?

Talk with others about their anger. Ask them what they get angry about. Ask them how they express their anger. Compare patterns. You'll find out you are not alone.

Make a list of all the things you could have been angry about as a child. Example:

- I could have been angry with my dad for hitting my mom when she was drunk.
- I could have been angry with my dad for giving my dog away.
- I could have been angry with my mom the time she passed out on Christmas Eve.
- I could have been angry with my mom for not listening to me when I told her dad was drunk.

Now, make a list of things that as an adult you could be angry about but aren't.

Example:

- I could be angry with my dad for never getting sober.
- I could be angry with my sister for never going to see my mom.
- I could be angry with my husband for not being more willing to listen to me when I want to talk about my mom or dad.
- I could be angry when I think people have taken advantage of me.

When you have approximately four or five examples of situations in which you could be angry as a child or adult, draw a large "X" across the words "I could have been" and "I could be" in every one of those sentences. Then write, "I am," "I was," or "I am still," depending on whether or not you are still angry.

Example:

- I am still angry with my dad for hitting my mom when she was drunk.
- I am angry with my dad for never getting sober.
- I am still angry with my dad for giving my dog away.
- I was angry with my mom the time she passed out on Christmas Eve.
- I am angry when I think people have taken advantage of me.
- I am still angry with my mom for not listening to me when I told her Dad was drunk.
- I am angry with my husband for not being more willing to listen to me when I want to talk about my mom or dad.

Now, reflect on those sentences and thoughts—be aware of how you feel.

If you are working on this exercise with someone, tell him or her how you feel. Is it difficult to admit your feelings? Some of you will find relief in simply acknowledging past pain. Others won't like the feelings at all. Remember, acknowledging anger, as well as other feelings, is a necessary part of the recovery, and the more you share your experiences with yourself and with others, the more comfortable recovery will be for you. A secondary benefit is an increased closeness and bond with those friends with whom you choose to share your feelings.

Recognizing and challenging anger constructively will allow you to identify your needs. Anger will help you identify limits and boundaries you need to set. When owned and expressed constructively, it will give you the courage to be self-caring.

Guilt

Imagine holding on to guilt about something over which you had absolutely no control, Imagine doing that for ten, twenty, thirty years, possibly a lifetime. When children take on guilt for things they are not responsible for they invariably continue to add more and more guilt to an already existing load.

I met Charlie when he was seventy-four years old. He came to me asking if I would participate in a task force for a local helping agency. After he had introduced himself and told me about the needs of the agency, he admitted he was not familiar with my work but had been told by others that I worked with kids whose parents are alcoholics.

I acknowledged the information he had been given was correct, and I began explaining the nature of what I do. I had been speaking for only about three to four minutes when he interrupted me suddenly, saying, "Yeah . . . yeah . . . my dad was alcoholic. Uh, he died." His gaze dropped from my eyes, and he began looking fixedly at the floor. "Yeah," he said. "I was thirteen." His gaze turned to the ceiling. "He was thirty-one or thirty-two, I guess. Died in an accident. He was drunk when it happened." Haltingly, he continued, "You know, I never understood. I never understood. You know I tried to be good. I never knew what he wanted though. I know I did things he didn't like, but I wasn't a bad kid."

Charlie had carried his guilt for sixty-one years. He was not rambling in semi-senility, he was feeling pure guilt. He still believed he was responsible for his father's drinking and, ultimately, his father's death. He had carried all these years of guilt because he had no understanding of the disease process.

James told me, "I have carried guilt feelings throughout my life because I didn't want the responsibility of raising my brother and sisters. I deserted my mom when I was eighteen and joined the army. I deserted her—just like my alcoholic father."

For one and a half years in Al-Anon, Julie, age thirty-five, has been seriously addressing her issues around guilt. "I have a lot of issues to deal with about my mother—her constant criticism, guilt because I didn't know why I was being criticized, and finally, my guilt for being alive."

People need to reassess those things for which they held themselves responsible. The Serenity Prayer, which is the hallmark philosophy of Alcoholics Anonymous and Al-Anon, says,

God grant me the serenity
To accept the things I cannot change,
The courage to change the things I can,
And the wisdom to know the difference.

The more you understand, the easier it is to accept that you aren't responsible for your parents' addiction or their behaviors. It is important you realize that as a young child you had only emotional, psychological, and physical capabilities to behave as just that—a child. Once you have accepted that, it is easier not to be so self-blaming and guilt ridden.

Think about the guilt you still carry. Do you ever say, "If only I had . . . "? Take some time right now to examine your guilt feelings by working the following exercise.

- As a child, if only I had . . .
- As a teenager, if only I had . . .

Now, seriously answer, would any other six-year-old, twelve-year-old, or eighteen-year-old in the same situation, with the same circumstances, have behaved any differently? In fact, even as a twenty-five-year-old or a thirty-five-year-old, without knowledge of addiction and its many ramifications, would it be possible to respond differently? As an adult, the tendency to accept all guilt is a pattern that needs to be broken.

Ask yourself:

- What did I do with my guilt as a child?
- Was I forever apologizing?
- Was I a perfect child making up for what I thought I was doing wrong?

It is important to gain a realistic perspective of situations that you have the power to affect. Adult children often have a distorted perception of where their power lies and as a result live with false guilt. *True guilt* is remorse or regret we feel for something we have done or did not do. *False guilt* is taking responsibility for someone else's behavior and actions.

Because this is usually a lifelong habit, it is important to go back and delineate historically what you were and were not responsible for. That will assist you in being more skilled in recognizing a lifelong pattern of taking on false guilt and stopping it.

Rewrite the following sentence stems and fill in the blanks. Write "No," in the first blank, and then continue by finishing the sentence:

_____ I was not responsible for _____
when he/she did _____ .

_____ it wasn't my fault when _____
_____ .

_____ it wasn't my duty or obligation to _____
_____ .

Then take the time to write about anything else you might feel guilty about that wasn't your fault. When people feel guilty, many times they end up crying, looking as if they are sad or disappointed, or twisting the guilt into anger. Disguising one's true feelings by putting up a false front is a common practice. Out of the need to survive, people will create distorted expressions of feelings.

What do you feel guilty about?
- Little things in everyday life.
- Everything in everyday life.

What do you do when you feel guilty?
- Buy presents for the person toward whom you feel the guilt.
- Get depressed.
- Get angry.
- Berate yourself.

When you are feeling guilt, a simple exercise is to ask yourself:
- What did I do to affect the situation?
- What can I do to make it any different?
- Can I accept that I did all that I was able to do with the resources available?

Give yourself permission to make mistakes. Take responsibility for what is yours, but don't accept responsibility for what is not. You will need to work on your self-image and your ability to understand and express your own fear and anger, as well as to learn ways to deal with your guilt.

The possibilities for masking feelings are many. Anxiety, depression, overeating, insomnia, oversleeping, high blood pressure, overwork, always being sick, always being tired, being overly nice—the list goes on. These consequences affect not only your life, but they interfere with your relationships with others—your spouse, your lover, your children, your friends. Now is the time to change the pattern, but please don't try to do it in a vacuum. Let others be a part of this new growth.

Recovery is the ability to tolerate feelings without the need to medicate or engage in other self-defeating behaviors.

Daughters of the Bottle

until i was twenty-two
i didn't think anyone else had a drunk for a mother
then i met lori joannie and susan
i recognized them immediately by their stay away smiles
they were leaders in their work
competent imposters like me who would say they were sorry
if somebody bumped into them on a crowded street
i call on them once in a while
they always come
children of alcoholics always do.
Jane

Breaking the Don't Trust Rule

When you grow up not being able to trust the most significant people in your life it is difficult to trust others. At the same time it is possible there were trustworthy people at moments or possibly even throughout your growing-up years. The following exercises will help you begin to explore the issue of trust.

On a continuum from one to ten, one being totally non-trusting of people to ten, which is trusting everyone, where would you place yourself today.

Circle the answer to the following sentence stem:

"In my growing-up years, I could trust my . . ." If there was more than one, be specific with the name.

Father	Brother
Mother	Sister
Stepparent	Friend
Grandparent	Other: _____

When completed, for those you circled write a few sentences as to what it was about them made them trustworthy.

Complete the sentence:
Today I struggle with trusting people because . . .

The opposite side of the continuum is that sometimes in a search for love and acceptance adult children trust and put faith in people who are not honest and not reliable. If you identify, describe.

When you have become accustomed to only trusting yourself it can be difficult to be trusting of others. Yet there is a void in this one-sided approach to life. Make a list, even if short, of the benefits to trusting others.

As much as you may not think you trust others, it is very possible there are people in your life that you trust in certain ways. You don't have to think of trust as an all-or-nothing attribute, there are people you would trust in some areas but not others. There are people who are trustworthy at certain times but not others. You do need to discriminate the ways in which and with whom you are trusting. There may be certain people at work you trust to help you out with specific projects. There may be a neighbor you trust to help you when your car is broken down and you need a ride. There may be a friend in the twelve-step community who you trust to hold a confidence. You trust your therapist to be respectful as he or she listens to you when you feel vulnerable.

Make a list of the situations and the people who you have found trustworthy.

Reshaping Roles

Responsible Child

The responsible child, otherwise known as the nine-year-old going on thirty-five, has probably come to find him- or herself as very organized and goal-oriented. The responsible child is adept at planning and manipulating others to get things accomplished, allowing him or her to be in a leadership position. He or she is often independent and self-reliant, capable of accomplishments and achievements. But because these accomplishments are made less out of choice and more out of a necessity to survive (emotionally, if not physically), there is usually a price paid for this early maturity.

For example: "As a result of being the little adult in my house, I didn't have time to play baseball because I had to make dinner for my sisters."

Complete the following:

As a result of being the little adult in my house, I didn't have time to
_____ because _____ .

As a result of being the little adult in my house, I didn't have time to
_____ because _____ .

As a result of being the little adult in my house, I didn't have time to
_____ because _____ .

As a result of being the little adult in my house, I didn't have time to
_____ because _____ .

For the person who has the ability to accomplish a great deal, the issue of control often creates problem areas in adult life. Accompanying a strong need to be in control is an extreme fear of being totally out of control, particularly with feelings. As Sue said, "If I permitted myself to throw one plate out of frustration, there would be nothing stopping me from throwing thirty!"

Because so much of life has been lived in extremes, you feel as if you are in control or out of control. You don't know about *some* control. View it as impossible as being a little bit pregnant. Perceiving control to be an all-or-nothing experience, of course you don't want to give it up. It once protected you. Giving up control is frightening because it has been vital to your safety. Control of the external forces in the environment is a survival mechanism. It is self-protection. It may be what allowed you to make sense out of your life. Controlling behavior was an attempt to bring order and consistency into inconsistent and unpredictable family situations. It is a defense against shame. Feeling in control gives a sense of power when overwhelmed by powerlessness, helplessness, and fear. Giving up control as an adult is difficult when up to this point in life it has been of great value.

- Sit back in a comfortable seat and relax. Breathe deeply.
- Uncross your legs and arms. Gently close your eyes and reflect back in time to your growing-up years.
- Recognizing how you exerted control externally or internally, finish this sentence:

Giving up control in my family would have meant _____.
Giving up control in my family would have meant _____.
Giving up control in my family would have meant _____.
Giving up control in my family would have meant _____.
Giving up control in my family would have meant _____.

If you have difficulty with this exercise, another way to benefit from it is to describe the controlling behavior. Remember, controlling behavior was developed to protect you, so don't be judgmental.

For example:

Not taking care of my mother would have meant

_____ .

—or—

Not doing the grocery shopping would have meant

_____ .

—or—

Not holding in my feelings would have meant

_____ .

Repeating these sentences allows you to access a deeper level of honesty. Now ask yourself if control means the same thing to you today.

As you become aware of the frightening connotation that the issue of control has, it is equally important to remind yourself of the positive aspects that come with letting go of some control. It is in giving up *some* control that you genuinely become empowered.

In asking those in recovery to name what they experienced as they let go of control they responded:

Peace, serenity.	*Spontaneity.*
Relaxation.	*Creativity.*
Ability to listen to others.	*Fun, play.*
Ability to listen to myself.	*Energy.*
Trust in myself.	*My present feelings.*
Lack of fear.	*Intimacy with self and others.*

These are the rewards, the promises of recovery.

As you reshape your life, you can retain pride in your ability to accomplish, but you also need to develop a greater sense of spontaneity and a greater ability to interact with others in a less rigid manner. You will be able to give up some areas of control only after you learn to identify your feelings and express these feelings in a manner that feels safe to you.

Adjuster

The adjusting child finds it easier not to question, think about, nor respond in any way to what was occurring in his or her life. Adjusters do not attempt to change, prevent, or alleviate any situations. They simply adjust to what they are told, often by detaching themselves emotionally, physically, and socially as much as is possible.

While it is easier to survive the frequent confusion and hurt of a dysfunctional home through adjusting, there are many negative consequences in adult life.

Example: "As a result of adjusting/detaching, I got into a lot of strange situations because I didn't stop to think."

Complete the following:

As a result of adjusting/detaching, I _____

_____

because _____

_____ .

As a result of adjusting/detaching, I _____

_____

because _____

_____ .

As a result of adjusting/detaching, I _____

_____

because _____

_____ .

As a result of adjusting/detaching, I _____

_____

because _____

_____ .

The children who are more detached, possibly more nondescript than the responsible, placating, or acting-out children, are the adjusters. They need to take a look at how they feel about themselves. Adjusters have operated on the premise that life is easier if you don't draw attention to yourself. They need to give themselves new messages that communicate that they are important people, and they deserve attention because they are important, they have value. Adjusters have many feelings that they have not had the opportunity to examine and feelings that they have not had the opportunity to share with others.

Adjusting adults continue to survive usually by living their lives in a very malleable fashion. They need to recognize that at times it is healthier and more satisfying to be less flexible. Because adjusters make very few waves for other people, they have no sense of direction for themselves. They lack purpose or a feeling of fulfillment. It is like always just being along for the ride—one feels a sense of movement, yet often travels only in circles.

One adult child revealed that her husband decided to move five times, taking her to five states, in the first four years of their marriage. She said she didn't realize she could have discouraged any of the moves and, in fact, could have refused to go. She said she always did what he wanted. In retrospect, her adjusting was not good for her husband or for their relationship. If you are such an adjusting adult, you need daily practice in identifying the power you have in your life. Here is a four-part exercise that will help you do just that.

Part 1. At the beginning of each day, write down at least five options you have that day.

For example:
1. I choose whether or not I eat breakfast.
2. I choose where I buy gas for the car.
3. I choose whom I sit with at lunch.
4. I choose which television show I watch.
5. I choose the time I go to bed.

Recognize that these five options are certainly not major decisions, but in the beginning, it is wise to start with the small areas of daily life one can change. This exercise should be done consistently for a period of one week.

Part 2. Continue this exercise for a second week, listing ten choices that can be made on a daily basis. The goal of this exercise is to teach you to acknowledge your power in making choices. By the third or fourth day, you will begin to feel the power.

Part 3. After following through with Part 2, practice on a daily basis making notes of existing options that were not acted upon. List three per day. Continue this part of the exercise for one week.

For example:
1. I did not speak up when I was shortchanged $1.60 at the grocery store.
2. I allowed my daughter to use the car for the evening when I wanted to use it.
3. I didn't tell my friends I disliked Japanese food when they suggested we eat at a sushi restaurant for my birthday.

The purpose of Part 3 is to recognize situations in which you did not act on your power.

Part 4. After each day's documentation, make a log of what could be done differently should the situation occur again. Even if you do not take that different action, list a few alternative responses. Should other alternatives not come to mind, another person—a friend, a therapist, someone who you respect—may be able to recommend an option.

Practice Parts 3 and 4 together for another week. They can be repeated as often as you feel the need. Discuss this process with another, share the fun of having so many choices, and allow yourself to feel some pride in this new awareness.

If you are an adjuster who is attempting to change, watch for certain clues. Should you begin to experience boredom, depression, or a sense of helplessness, it is time to become reacquainted with your power and options. Practice the previous exercise again.

Placater

The placater, otherwise known as the household social worker or caretaker, is the child busy taking care of everyone else's emotional needs. This may be the young girl who perceives her sister's embarrassment when Mom shows up at a school open house drunk and will do whatever is necessary to take the embarrassment away This may be a boy assisting his brother in not feeling the disappointment of Dad not showing up at a ball game. This is the child who intervenes and assures that his siblings are not too frightened after there has been a screaming scene between their parents. This is a warm, sensitive, listening, caring young person who shows a tremendous capacity to help others feel better. For the placater, survival was taking away the fears, sadness, and guilt of others. Survival was giving one's time, energy, and empathy.

But as adults, people who have spent years taking care of others begin to "pay a price" for the "imbalance of focus." It is most likely that there were things that were not learned.

Example: "As a result of being the household social worker, I didn't have time to tell anyone my problems because I was too busy assisting in solving other people's problems."

Complete the following:

As a result of being the household social worker, I didn't have time to

_____

because _____

_____ .

As a result of being the household social worker, I didn't have time to

_____

because _____

_____ .

As a result of being the household social worker, I didn't have time to

_____

because _____

_____ .

As a result of being the household social worker, I didn't have time to

_____

because _____

_____ .

For adult children who spend so much time taking care of other people's needs, it is important to understand the word selfish. They have perfected the inability to give to themselves or consider their own needs. The placater's role is always to attend to the feelings and wants of another. As adult placaters proceed in recovery, it is natural for them to feel guilty for focusing on themselves.

> *When I decide to put myself first for a change, I feel very guilty and have trouble differentiating between putting myself first and being selfish.*

Remember, you are learning how to give to yourself and that is not bad. In order to be willing to give to yourself, it is vital to look at old messages that may need to be changed.

New messages may be:

- I don't have to take care of everyone else.
- I have choices about how I respond to people.
- My needs are important.
- I have feelings; I'm scared; I am angry.
- It is okay to put my own well-being first.
- Some situations can be resolved without my being involved.
- Others can lend support to those who need it when I am not willing to be available.
- I'm not guilty because others feel bad.

This should only be the beginning of a list of new messages. To the adult placater, make a list of new messages. On a daily basis for a minimum of a month, read and reread these messages aloud to yourself.

You will feel some of the old guilt for a while, but it will be mixed with a new sensation—that of excitement along with a sense of aliveness. I believe in people giving themselves credit and being their own best friend so do not be embarrassed about validating yourself.

Fifty-four-year-old Maureen said she spent her life trying to be everybody's good little girl. She walked a very narrow line, afraid to do anything that might cause anyone's disapproval. "Slowly, I have learned it is much more important for me to consider my own needs and feelings, and how important it is for me to act on them." This is the type of freedom all adult children can attain. Maureen knows the process is slow. It is not easy to give up fears and try new behaviors. But, it is possible!

If you think you fit into the placater's role, examine how you give. On a daily basis, document all the little things you do for people. Itemize each one. After you have read your list of anywhere from fifty to a hundred items, are you tired? Of course you are tired. Where will you find the energy to give to yourself? The answer—you won't. Ask yourself if each of these placating acts was absolutely necessary. Could you have backed off a little? As you attempt to back off on giving, you need to start work on being able to receive. All true placaters need to work on receiving.

Ask yourself about your capacity to receive. Do you "yes, but . . ." when you are complimented? Do you change the subject when you are commended? Are you embarrassed or do you feel awkward when you receive a gift? Can you enjoy the moment? You may need to give yourself new messages regarding receiving:

- I deserve to be given a thank-you.
- I can enjoy being the recipient of praise.
- I will take time to hear my praise, smile, and soak it in.

For a minimum of two weeks, pay strict attention to receiving. Practice your new messages.

Mascot

Humor and wit are valuable characteristics. Everyone appreciates laughter and the relief and distraction it can provide at times. But when it is the predominant way of being, the primary coping mechanism, you don't get to learn or experience things that would be helpful to you.

For example, "As a result of being the family clown, I didn't have time to pay attention at school."

Complete the following:

As a result of my mascot/clown role, I didn't have time to

_____
_____
_____ .

As a result of my mascot/clown role, I didn't have time to

_____
_____
_____ .

As a result of my mascot/clown role, I didn't have time to

_____
_____
_____ .

Another sentence stem exercise that may be of value for insight:

My humor covered my _____ .
My humor covered my _____ .
My humor covered my _____ .

Or

Letting go of my humor would have meant _____ .
Letting go of my humor would have meant _____ .
Letting go of my humor would have meant _____ .

Acting-Out Child

Acting-out children are confused and scared and act out their confusion in ways that get them a lot of negative attention. Some kids became very angry at a young age. They get into trouble at home, school, and often on the streets. These are kids screaming, "There's something wrong here!" These are kids who didn't find survivorship in the other three roles.

Example: "As a result of my acting-out behavior, I didn't have time to pay attention at school."

Complete the following:

As a result of my acting-out behavior, I didn't have time to

_____
_____
_____ .

As a result of my acting-out behavior, I didn't have time to

_____
_____
_____ .

As a result of my acting-out behavior, I didn't have time to

_____
_____
_____ .

As a result of my acting-out behavior, I didn't have time to

_____
_____
_____ .

It is easy to scapegoat yourself for being in this role, yet creativity, flexibility, honesty, and humor are but a few of the strengths often shown by people who adopted this stance. Make a list of characteristics you value about yourself. If they are not taken to an extreme, they are most likely strengths.

Adult Roles

Today as an adult I am still (check the appropriate boxes):

☐ Overly responsible
☐ Placating
☐ Adjusting
☐ Using humor as a defense
☐ Acting out negatively
☐ Other _____

As a result, I still haven't learned

_____
_____
_____ .

It is important for me to take the time to (be specific)

_____
_____
_____ .

Letter of Thanks

It is important to honor your coping mechanisms; they were critical to your survivorship. Recovery doesn't involve being critical of what you needed to do to protect yourself while you were growing up.

Whatever your predominant role was, write a letter to it thanking it for how it was helpful at the time.

Then go on to tell that role how it ultimately got in your way or caused you problems as an adult.

Dear (role),

I want to thank you for _____ .

But there were things I didn't get to do or didn't get to learn because of you.

I didn't _____

_____

_____

_____ .

Honoring the Strengths of the Roles

Review the strengths and vulnerabilities of the roles you identify with and note the personal strengths that you want to maintain.

Establishing Boundaries

Circle the boundary violations that you experienced growing up.

- Parents do not view you as separate beings from themselves and want you to meet their needs.
- Parents did not take responsibility for their feelings, thoughts, and behaviors but expected you to take responsibility for them.
- Parents' self-esteem is derived totally through your behavior.
- You were treated as a peer with no parent/child distinction.
- Parents expect you to fulfill their dreams.
- Parents objectify you as a possession, as a belonging versus as your own human entity with rights and desires

By establishing boundaries and setting limits, you will begin to find the freedom of using the words "No" and "Yes." It was not safe to say no as a child. Without the freedom to say no, yes was said with tremendous fear and helplessness or out of a desperate need for approval and love. Recovery means recognizing the ability to say no is a friend to protect you. You have the power and right to say no and yes. You will find that yes is a gift that is offered freely rather than out of fear or the need for approval. Recognize that by saying no, you are actually saying yes to yourself.

Make a list of people you would like to set better boundaries with, identify what that boundary would look or sound like. Note if you need support and where you can get that support.

	Names	Boundary	Support Source
1.	_____	_____	_____
2.	_____	_____	_____
3.	_____	_____	_____
4.	_____	_____	_____
5.	_____	_____	_____

Start with the one who feels most safe to you and one you think you will be most successful.

Getting to Know Your Trauma

Circle the traumas you experienced on a chronic basis:

- Severe criticism and blaming.
- Verbal abuse.
- Broken promises.
- Lying.
- Unpredictability.
- Rage.
- Harsh or even cruel forms of punishment.
- Being forced into physically dangerous situations such as being in a vehicle with an impaired driver.
- Parental indifference to your needs and wants.
- Emotional unavailability, not showing love and concern.
- Unrealistic expectations.
- Disapproval is aimed at your entire being, your identity, your worth, and value rather than a particular behavior.

Trauma Timeline

To get another visual, you can pull the trauma, roles, and shame-based beliefs into one piece of work.

You will need a large piece of paper and different colored pencils. Draw a line across the page. On the left write birth, and to the far right end note your age today. See below.

Birth _____ Today

Along the line, begin by noting the traumas you experienced (you may want to refer to the traumas identified in the previous exercise and/ or those discussed in Chapter Five). If it is chronic such as rejection for your sexual orientation or unrealistic expectations, note the age you first experienced it and then draw a continuous line that shows how long it continued.

With a different color pencil, note approximate age when your predominant family role began to show itself. Then note if that role ever shifted in your growing-up years.

Under each trauma, identify the beliefs you internalized about yourself.

For example:

I am a bad person. I hate myself. Nothing I do is okay.

Taking Risks

List five risks you have taken in the past that you feel good about. They could be risks at work, in your family, or as a part of a love relationship. Name the risk. What did you fear? What did you do, say, or think to get yourself to push through the fear and take the risk?

	Risk	Fear	Push
1.	_____	_____	_____
2.	_____	_____	_____
3.	_____	_____	_____

4. _____ _____ _____
5. _____ _____ _____

Many people attempting to make changes sometimes fear they will go to the other extreme. While the internal experience may feel extreme, the behavior is usually not. What often feels internally like the roar of a lion is only a peep. It's just that for you it is alien, and it feels intense. There is a saying that I have appreciated over the years: "Feel the fear and do it anyway." You need to push through the fear. And you have begun to do that. You are breaking the rules of Don't Talk, Don' t Feel, and Don't Trust. Recovery is occurring.

CHAPTER EIGHT

The Child within the Home

Children are not immune from the effects of addiction. They live with it and therefore need to understand it. First and foremost they need to know the 7 Cs.

> ### The Seven "C"s
>
> I didn't **CAUSE** it.
>
> I can't **CONTROL** it.
>
> I can't **CURE** it, but
>
> I can help take **CARE** of myself by
>
> **COMMUNICATING** my feelings,
>
> Making healthy **CHOICES**,
>
> and
>
> **CELEBRATING** me.
>
> © Jerry Moe, MA

I Didn't Cause It

Children often blame themselves for family problems, sometimes they are told it is their fault by family members. When children experience trauma in their lives and no one explains it to them in an age-appropriate way, they make up a story for it all to make sense. They are often not only dealing with addiction but also other problems that may be associated with it such as divorce, domestic violence, depression, incarceration. Children need to hear that they did not cause their parents addiction; they did not cause their parent's depression; they are not responsible for their parents not being together. They are not responsible for the problems their parents are experiencing. And they need to hear this over and over and over.

I Can't Control It

Children may take steps to stop a parent's drinking or using. They vigorously attempt to improve things in their families. Some pour alcohol down the drain and throw away drugs they find hidden in the house. Others take on parental responsibilities that often include caring for their brothers and sisters. Some play the peacemaker during times of conflict. They may try to be perfect in all they do hoping all of these behaviors will help the problems go away. When this does not work they simply try harder.

It is vital to teach children that addiction is a disease. Once the person who is addicted starts drinking or using, he or she cannot stop. Children understand the words "stuck," "being hooked," or "trapped." It is also essential to explain that people suffering from addiction are not bad. Yet when they are stuck, hooked, and trapped, they sometimes do bad things like breaking promises, not playing with their kids, or maybe even not coming home. It is important to help children separate the people they love from the disease that consumes their parent.

Understanding addiction also reduces their anxiety by making the unexpected predictable. Knowing that the family is responding to a sickness allows the child to remain guilt-free because an illness is not something they can cause or control. When children realize a parent is addicted, it gives them the freedom to filter and evaluate the information passed along. Most significantly, it gives a name to their experience, and it says they aren't at fault. It gives them a voice with which to talk about their experiences.

Children who grow up never having shared their closest thoughts or feelings with even their very best friend, live a very lonely, isolated way of life. This loneliness continues into adulthood because no one understood their trauma or was willing to take the time to talk to them. When the dysfunctional family rules are broken, children have a foundation for understanding what they are experiencing.

If the concepts of addiction are explained in age-appropriate language they understand, children of all ages can comprehend it. Adults need to talk openly and provide children with access to resources that reinforce healthy messages.

Disease of Addiction

It is advisable to ask children how they would describe addiction and what traits constitute being an alcoholic or addict. Children have undoubtedly heard the stories from a friend, a family member, or through the media that are often inaccurate portrayals filled with judgment and stigma. Asking the child for his or her perception offers the helping person an opportunity to gauge, clarify, or validate knowledge.

Addiction is not a disease caused by a germ or virus, as are many others, but it is an illness nonetheless. People do not choose to become addicted and all the willpower in the world will not control or cure addiction. Children prior to the ages of nine and ten do not need a lot of explanation. They are more accepting of it being a disease with both phyiscal and psychological ramifications. It makes sense to them. They more readily accept the analogy of being stuck to something and not being able to get off, such as having gum stuck in your hair and needing help to get it out; a fish stuck on a hook and needing a person to unhook it; a bee stuck to a flower. Often they are told a parent is allergic to alcohol or other drugs and the allergy makes the brain work differently and the parent does things he or she wouldn't do otherwise. The only way to stop is to totally stop using altogether. But because the brain is confused, the parent needs help from others to stop. Children see the personality changes and also see the inability to stop once started. With young children, this conversation is more likely to be brief and more general.

As young people move into their adolescent and adult years they are not so willing to accept the disease model as an answer for why or how their parent behaves. They are often angry and perceive the disease model as a cop out. It's still helpful for them to be given an education about addiction. It will not be lost on them. With this older child it is also helpful to discuss the role denial played in the disease, describe the progression of losing control, how the addict is responsible for relapses and, if experienced, what was learned from the relapse. In the long run it will be changing behaviors that will heal relationships with their children of all ages.

Blackouts

Blackouts are periods of amnesia, varying in duration from minutes to several hours or, for some people, several days. It is a period of time when a person is under the influence of alcohol or other drugs—particularly benzodiazepines and barbiturates—yet is awake and interacting in the environment, possibly even socially engaged. However, the memory of the experience is not recorded in the brain and therefore the person is unable to remember what happened. Not all alcoholics or addicts will experience blackouts but should they occur they are very confusing and result in a lot of anxiety and anger.

Imagine a Friday night when Dad doesn't come home for dinner and still isn't home when everyone has gone to bed. When he finally does arrive, he makes a lot of noise and argues with his thirteen-year-old daughter, whom he meets in the hallway as she heads for the bathroom. Dad then proceeds to wake Mom and the two of them argue loudly for several hours in their bedroom. All three kids listen to the arguing throughout the night. The next day everyone acts as if none of that happened. Actually, the father doesn't know what happened. The last thing he remembers about Friday night is drinking with his friends and anticipating that his wife would be angry because he was late for dinner. His recollection of the night stops somewhere in the early evening. He doesn't remember when or even how he got home, arguing with his daughter, or with his wife. He does know he feels lousy and that his kids are acting skittish and his wife is angry but not talking. All of the children show some anxiety around him and are very apprehensive. Rather than risk knowing the reality of the previous night, after all that would confront his drinking behavior, he would feel fear, guilt, and shame, so he simply acts placating of everyone the rest of the day. No one talks about the real issues—Dad's behavior the night before, the confusion, the fear, and the disappointment. In a family already fragmented, more distance and misunderstanding are created.

Children are often hurt about events the addicted person doesn't even recall. It's extremely crazymaking. And seldom are there any related discussions, as the addicted person feels guilt and fear should he or she pursue finding out about those events. The partner feels confusion as the children do as well as feeling angry and hopeless. The children are just accumulating another painful experience leaving them with more fear, sadness, embarrassment and, at the least, confusion.

Some children may suspect that their parent, when drinking or using, actually does not remember a period of time. Other children who do not understand what is happening with their parent have an even greater sense of confusion and craziness. Whether or not children recognize when blackouts occur, they need to have some information and an explanation that validates their own experience and allows them to have a better understanding of their parent's behavior.

An analogy that may be useful is describing a blackout as a switch turning off one part of the brain and nothing is allowed to enter that part. When the switch comes back on, the part of the brain that was turned off remembers nothing that occurred during the time it was switched off.

Personality Changes

The Jekyll-and-Hyde personality is common in homes riddled with addiction. The alcoholic parent, when on the rising side of the blood alcohol curve often becomes more expansive in attitude, is more warm, welcoming, loving, generous, and then when on the downward side they are often are more agitated. Anyone who gets in the way of their using are targets for their agitation.

Drugs and alcohol impact volatility of emotions and influence lack of impulse control, which changes personality. The thinking part of the brain goes to sleep while the emotional part of the brain has begun to take over, the part that says, "I want what I want when I want it and don't get in my way."

Children also describe the nonaddicted parent as demonstrating personality changes. "We leave for school in the morning and mom is all nice and loving. When we come home she snaps at us the minute we come through the door. Then she disappears to suddenly be right back in the living room and is really angry. She tells us we are slobs, yelling that we need to get our homework done, that we aren't grateful enough. We don't know what was happening, she gets like that a lot. But mostly she is really nice to us. She makes us things, likes to be around us. It's so confusing." The codependent parent's preoccupation with the addict and the fluctuation of feelings associated creates unpredictability and irrational responses.

MY DADDY GOES AWAY SOMETIMES

AN UGLY STRANGER
CAME TO OUR HOUSE
WHEN DADDY DRANK.
I DON'T LIKE HIM
HE SCARES ME.

I WAS SO HAPPY
TO SEE MY DADDY
HAD COME BACK
THE NEXT MORNING
I WANT HIM TO STAY.
HE'S MY <u>REAL</u> DADDY.
I LOVE HIM SO MUCH.

SARAH 14

Broken Promises

Broken promises are a common reality for children living with addiction. They are often told they will be going someplace or a parent will attend a school event or they will be given something, only to have the parent not follow through. This usually occurs with no accountability or apology. It is important that children know their feelings are valid and that promises are broken because of the parent's addiction not because of a lack of caring or loving. Sadly, the preoccupation with drinking or using becomes the addict's number one priority. All else is secondary.

Denial

Denial occurs when people pretend things are different than they really are. In order to protect their addiction, addicts deny how much they drink or use and the impact this has on others. If the addicted person is not in denial he or she is faced with overwhelming shame, guilt, powerlessness, fear and hopelessness. That then leads back to denial.

My Mother hides Her Drinks

(But she doesn't hide them very well.)

age 11

Family members also deny. The partner and children deny for many of the same reasons. If they don't deny, the truth is too emotionally overwhelming. Without a sense of why, without direction, without hope, it's easier to move into denial. Children don't just deny what they see, they also deny their feelings, say things like "It didn't hurt," when it did; "I wasn't angry," when they were; " I wasn't embarrassed," when they were; "He didn't know what he was doing," when he did.

Multiple Addictions

Often by the time a person seeks recovery he or she is addicted to more than one behavior or substance. The family may or may not know that. The following analogies are helpful in explaining multiple addictive disorders.

If there are two or more addictions occurring at the same time, think of it as a wagon being pulled by a team of horses. Sometimes one horse pulls the wagon, representing a single addiction, but it could be two, three, or even four horses.

Another way to think of this is to get a car started you have to use the ignition. One addiction is the key in the ignition, the second addiction is the fuel in the tank.

Relapse

Relapses are not unusual in that they occur in most progressive diseases. In a disease such as cancer, there are times when the cancer appears to be in remission and is not progressing. Then, it may reappear again and the patient is said to have had a relapse. When someone has pneumonia and recovers, they may become sick again, suffering a relapse. Relapse is a term that needs to be discussed if a parent attempts to get clean and sober. Many parents ask, "Why worry the child?" The reality is the child is already worried. It is also possible he or she has already witnessed a relapse and are acutely aware it could happen again. To not discuss relapse is to stay in denial about its possibility.

Nine-year-old Melody described most eloquently a definition of relapse.

A relapse is when you stop drinking and then you start again. It's like when you have a cold and you think it is gone. Then you go out in the rain and your cold comes back.

It's important for children to understand they don't cause relapses. When the father relapses shortly after his sixteen-year-old son wrecked the family car, dad is responsible for the relapse. The father must learn to cope with such problems or uncomfortable feelings, without reaching for his drug. The addict is not responsible for having the disease but is responsible his or her recovery.

I Can't Cure It

A child can't cure addiction. The addicted person and the other parent must get help for themselves. This can include going to a treatment program, working with a counselor, attending self-help meetings, and/

or returning to their faith. People can find joy, peace, and serenity if they stay committed to ongoing recovery practices.

Addiction is chronic, and the abstinence from the drug or the self-defeating behavior is the first step to recovery. People find if they stay in recovery practice it helps them to be honest with themselves (the psychological aspect of the disease), it helps them avoid slipping into rationalization and denial. It allows them to stay accountable for their own behavior. And it allows them to give back to others seeking recovery, which fills a spiritual void. As said by one twelve-step member, " Meetings keep me vigilant and help me not become complacent about this disease that is just one drink or one toke or one snort away. Meetings help me like myself. Going to meetings is like putting money into a savings account and it earns interest. Going to meetings is my 'recovery interest.'"

Most importantly, it is the responsibility of the adult to get the help they need, it's the children's job to be children.

MY DADDY

I woke up one morning and he was gone he was gone my daddy and he would never be home again.
He was gone my daddy
the one who always showed his love the one who always understood, when she never would!
The one who always brushed my hair, combed and put ribbons in my hair
he was the one who picked me up when I fell and skinned my knee. Oh my daddy, my daddy.
I still remember all the things he taught me—but he was gone. And I was too young to understand he said they just didn't get along.
I hardly ever saw him,
my daddy who was always there, my daddy who always cared. It seemed he just didn't have time for me. But that was also ten years ago and I think

now I understand.
But there's still one question that remains. And that's—Why
Oh Lord, did this have to happen to me???
Why did my daddy have to go, and leave me all alone?
She says he's alcoholic, a person who has a disease and needs
help . . . But can only get it if he wants it.
He must admit to himself that he is sick and needs help. he
knows all this now and I do too.
Now it's too late, he's already gone.
He's remarried now and he has a new little princess who he
brushes, combs, and puts ribbons in her hair. But Lord this is
so unfair!!!
He is my daddy and he needs help!!!
But I feel so helpless Lord because
it seems he still doesn't have time for me. I love my daddy,
whom I hardly ever see.
And even more when I think about
how much he must Love Me—MY DADDY

—Renee, age 16

I Can Help Take Care of Myself

Mindfulness and grounding practices are wonderful forms of self-care and have the added benefit of lessening trauma responses as they calm the emotional part of the brain. Such practices are forms of crafts, such as bead work, pottery, knitting, crocheting, all types of art. Engaging in nature and spending time with animals are also nurturing. Whether it is structured or spontaneous, singing and dancing can be calming and grounding. Reading is another way of taking care of yourself. Today there are apps and books available for young children to practice yoga, breathing, and guided imagery that are all helpful to keep kids present in the moment and to cope with the stress they are subject to.

Self-care also comes in the form of healthy boundaries. When children understand they don't cause the family stress nor are they in a position to cure it, they are in a better position to have healthier boundaries. A healthy boundary is often demonstrated by behavior and is not necessarily verbalized. Knowing how and when to remove yourself from an uncomfortable or unsafe situation is an important boundary, such as removing yourself from the potential line of fire when the verbal abuse begins. Where can you go that is safe? What can you do to distract yourself? When you are able to demonstrate problem-solving skills and engage in healthy choices those are acts of self-care. The ability to communicate feelings, build connections with others, and celebrate yourself are also acts of self-care.

Communicating My Feelings

Children raised with addiction experience loss on a chronic basis. When children experience loss they enter a grief process, one similar to the grief processes other people experience when they lose a loved one due to death or when a loved one becomes incapacitated because of a serious illness.

The first state of grief is disbelief or denying the loss has really occurred. The disbelief may be nature's way of helping a person through this stage by deadening the pain, by giving a person time to absorb the facts. Unfortunately, with addiction, this grief process is much slower, occurring over a much longer time and in a much more subtle way. As a result, family members are often in a state of disbelief for a lengthy time.

With addiction, as time passes and the truth becomes more evident, the family begins to experience terror—the terror of the reality that a loved one is an addict. Usually, the next emotion following the terror is anger. "If you (the addict) really love me, how can you be like this?" Family members often feel guilt and each family member believes that in some way he or she is responsible. A son believes, "Maybe if I hadn't talked back, Dad wouldn't drink so much or be so angry all the time." A wife believes, "If I were a better wife, my husband wouldn't be sick." A husband believes, "Maybe if I had been home more . . ." Bargaining is practiced by family members when they elicit promises from the addict to control or stop his or her using. At other times, bargaining is self-imposed, "If I behave this way, maybe Mom will respond another way." For many children, bargaining is through prayer, "Please God, keep my mom and dad together. Don't let them fight so much. I promise I will be *real* good."

Finally, family members feel desperation and despair. They each feel alone with the problem. They feel all these terrible things are unique in their lives, that no one else could possibly understand their pain. They despair that there are no answers or solutions to the guilt they carry. This process and these feelings are common to all persons affected by addiction.

Families who try to run away from their feelings suffer longer. Often, they never recover from their grief, and it becomes a long-lasting depression. Families who face loss and the related feelings, become stronger and are able to begin growing, living full and satisfying lives.

A child can survive a family crisis as long as the child is told the truth and allowed to share the natural sequence of feelings experienced when he or she suffers. In addictive families, everyone suffers, and everyone suffers very much alone. Children often suffer from loneliness, fear, anger, and a multitude of other feelings that they have no way of understanding and they do not have the ability to express this lack of understanding.

Although the child may receive help to understand addiction, intellectual understanding will not erase the multitude of intense feelings they experience. Children can understand and feel at the same time. It is important for someone to explain that their feelings are perfectly normal. Children need to be able to say, "I was so embarrassed. I know she is sick, but she still embarrasses me and it hurts!" Or, "I'm sad because Mom is like she is. But, I'm also really angry, and I don't understand why she won't go for help!" All of these feelings are valid. Children need to know others will validate and listen to their feelings.

EVERY NIGHT BEFORE DINNER WHEN
DADDY GETS HOME, MOMMY AND DADDY FIGHT.
DADDY SAYS MOMMY SHOULDN'T HAVE
ANOTHER GLASS OF SHERRY.
MOMMY SAYS SHE'S ONLY HAD 2!

I WAIT AND CRY IN THE HALL. I
DON'T WANT THEM TO SEE ME.

Tracy 11

Sadness

Crying is a natural release of the emotion of sadness. Crying is difficult for many people. Those in addicted families usually do one of two things: they learn how not to cry or cry alone, silently.

Before a child can cry and feel okay about it, the child needs to be given healthy messages regarding all feelings. Children need to hear "It's okay to cry." "Crying can help you feel better." Other messages, such as "Boys shouldn't cry" and "Don't be a crybaby," need to be countered. Children also need models who can demonstrate that crying is not weak or shameful. Children need to hear that when adults hurt they, too, cry. And that when family members show each other their tears, it is often a time in which they can feel closer to each other. Aside from giving permission to cry, children need support to share their feelings with others. Ask children who they could tell about the times when they cry? Who do they trust enough to confide in? Who in the family do they trust to ask for comfort at such times? This is an important discussion.

I once worked with a brother and sister, six-year-old Chuck and nine-year-old Melody. Chuck was very open about not trusting his mother and his helplessness regarding her drinking. He talked about worrying a lot, and how when he cried and Melody would tell him to shut up. She would talk louder when he was speaking and would call him a crybaby. She was prepared to do just about anything she could to keep Chuck from crying and showing his feelings. Though there was only three years difference in their ages, Chuck and Melody were in different phases of handling their stress. It is important for adults to be aware of these varying stages of denial among children and how children interfere with or are supportive of each other's expressions of feelings. One child may be more open to expression of tears, while another is obviously angry; still another child appears more emotionally disconnected. Each child needs to have access to all of their feelings and have healthy avenues of expression.

Fear

While fear is a natural emotion for all children, it is, unfortunately, pervasive in an addictive family. A parent's drinking or using results in a lot of tension in the home, and it's important a child's fears are acknowledged and validated. Whether or not children express specific fears, parents, family, and friends need to validate that at times it is normal to be afraid. Many times, nothing can be done about what is creating the fear, yet acknowledging it can lessen the power. Expressing feelings develops closeness between parents and children and is helpful in decreasing the children's feelings of being overwhelmed by the emotions kept inside. Emotions become so much more powerful when they are not outwardly expressed. Keeping feelings hidden can cause a great deal more pain than is necessary.

Anger

Everyone experiences anger. Yet due to punishment, the possibility of rejection, or fear of abuse, many children are reticent to own or share their anger. It is extremely important for children to become aware of their frustrations and angers and then find ways to express them. Children's anger is only problematic when it has been stored and appropriate ways of expression have not been introduced.

Ask children what happens when family members get angry. Their responses will guide you in supporting healthy behavior or countering unhealthy expressions of anger. When nine-year-old Mason was asked what people in his family do with anger, he said, "Dad leaves the house. Mom drinks. Tommy goes outside. I'm not really angry." Mason was a very overweight young boy, and his description demonstrated how he had copied his mother's pattern for coping with anger while his brother copied his father's pattern. Two family members leave their anger behind, and two drink or eat to cope with it. None of them found a healthy way of coping with anger.

To feel safe in expressing anger, children need adults to help them discriminate where it is and is not safe to share those feelings. They need to know their anger will not cause them to lose their parent's love. For many, expressing anger has come to mean "If I show you I'm angry with you, you will withdraw your love." Children need to know what limits are placed on the expression of anger and what others perceive as appropriate responses to situations. They need to know their hurts and anger are important and should not be discounted. Children often discount problems in their own lives because they believe problems within the family take precedence over any personal conflicts occurring outside the home. "Who am I to talk about how angry I became at school today? There is already enough tension at home." The messages learned are:

- What happened to me at school is not important.
- The feelings I have throughout the day are not important.
- I am not important.

Children need to have their feelings validated.

Guilt

Children assume they have the power to affect everything, when in truth, they have very little power in an addictive environment. "Dad was always screaming and hollering about us kids never doing anything right, so I assumed we had to be making him very unhappy and that was why he took off and didn't come home." Children need to know they do not cause someone to be addicted. Children need to be reassured that even if they behave in a way that upsets a parent their parent has many choices other than drinking or using to handle the situation. Remind them no one but the addict is responsible for the alcoholic/addict's actions.

It is important for a child to be able to distinguish the difference between true and false guilt. As stated previously, true guilt is a feeling of regret or remorse for your own behavior. For example, a person is responsible for being late, lying, stealing, not following through on a commitment. False guilt is a feeling of remorse that come from believing you are responsible for someone else's behavior and actions.

Devon is twenty-three years old. He recently attempted to take his own life, struggling with depression for a long time. He, his brothers, and his mother were all the recipients of his dad rages and verbal assaults. They were always being blamed for things; often called names. Devon never once talked back to his dad, never once tried to defend himself or his mom; he just accepted the abuse. He wanted to love his dad, but he was quietly becoming more and more angry. One day he had been bullied at school by some older boys, then came home to his dad's bullying. That night, he flew into a rage, yelling at his father, and started hitting him in the chest. Devon told him he was a lousy father and hoped he would go away and never come back. He didn't talk to his father the next couple days and then his father, while on a binge, got into a car accident; a passenger was killed and his father was sent to prison for the next several years. Devon felt that he "willed" his dad to get in that accident and has never forgiven himself. He has lived with this false guilt for over ten years. When you feel such futility, as Devon did, it is a normal response to wish that the person who creates so much pain would disappear, go away, and, yes, maybe even die. Instead of being able to be angry with his father and be sad for the relationship he may never have and for all the pain that has occurred, Devon implodes with guilt that is not his, fueling major depression that ultimately leads him to suicidality.

Love

Love consists of mutual respect, trust, and sharing. It is understandable for children to be confused about loving a parent who is frightening, unavailable, or inconsistent. Yet they learned early in childhood that they are expected to love and respect their parents. As a result, many children are ambivalent and confused about loving their parents.

Love frequently withstands a lot of inconsistent, painful parenting though. The love that is felt often relates to the experiences shared prior to the onset of addiction, as well as to the sober moments shared. Addicted parents are not under the influence all the time.

Remember, addiction is a process, the onset of which most often begins in young adulthood. This indicates that most parents begin raising their children prior to the addiction or in their early addictive years. When a person is in the early stages of addiction, the behavior may not be consistently disruptive to the family. The same is true for the nonaddicted parent. The codependent behavior was not necessarily typical of them in the early stages. They, too, were often more consistent and provided more quality time for the children. It is over time that nonaddicted parents become depressed, angry, rigid, or absent The love children feel was often internalized in those earlier years.

It is my bias that while we cannot make children love their parents, we can help them not to hate if we can provide more consistency in their lives, as well as educating them to better understand addiction and its effects on the entire family structure.

Learning to Feel

Children learn about feelings and what to do with them by modeling adults. The more healthy role models that are available, the greater the ability children have to adopt that healthy behavior and utilize positive avenues of expression. The more isolated the family becomes, the fewer options children have to learn from healthy adults. Children need access to healthy role models.

Children have to be helped to understand that feelings are transitory. One may feel intense hatred for a person, then, at another time, feel empathy and love. You may experience great tenderness one moment and only a few hours later feel enraged. Feelings change, and children will not be stuck with any one feeling forever.

They need to know it is possible to experience more than one feeling at a time. Love and hate, and sadness and anger can be felt together, as can happiness and sadness, fear and anxiety. There are numerous combinations. What's important is that the adult accepts the child's feelings. If adults can accept and validate children's feelings of intense dislike, as well as anger, fear, and disappointment, then they can also help children to live lives free of guilt for having these feelings. We can help children work through these feelings and, hopefully, acquire a more loving acceptance of themselves.

Making Healthy Choices

A part of making healthy choices is learning it is okay to ask for help. Children can only do that though if they have identified safe people in their life. Safe people could be extended family members, neighbors, friends' parents, school personnel ranging from coaches to teachers, to administrators, neighbors, etc.

Wendy needed to her mom to take her to an important school event but her mother was nearly passed out on the couch. Remembering she had learned about options at school, Wendy thought about her options: 1) not going; 2) going with a very impaired mother; 3) calling a friend and asking her mother to come and take her; 4) jogging to the event; or 5) calling her grandfather and asking him to take her. She called her grandfather. She knew he'd be more available than the friends' mom and knew she could be honest with him. She didn't want to be honest with the friends' mom, it was too embarrassing and she had to focus on the event. She knew she wouldn't get there if she jogged. She also knew her mom was too impaired to drive.

There are not any clear-cut satisfactory answers for such problems. All children need an adult, preferably a parent, to

- Offer them guidance and suggestions so children realize they have options.
- Protect them.
- Give them permission to protect themselves.

- Let them know it is okay to ask others for help.

Children can better handle problems and protect themselves when they have the time to discuss and think over potential situations. When they are briefed on possible situations, options identified, given positive messages about themselves, and believe an adult will support them, they will usually choose better options.

Celebrating Me

Every child is precious and deserves to be celebrated. Find ways to acknowledge, validate, and celebrate children. Acknowledge their problem-solving abilities. Acknowledge their creativity, talents, and personality attributes such as kindness and humor. Offer opportunities for them to show their strengths, be it on the playground, during visits to a friend's home or the classroom. You don't have to expect children to say thank you. They may even try to rebuff your feedback. Regardless, acknowledge, validate, and celebrate. It will make a difference.

Encourage Connections

Children grow up to be just like their parents or to have a variation of their parents' dysfunction unless someone shows them a different way. It is important for children to have a connection to others who help them problem-solve so they aren't problem-solving in a vacuum. They need someone who engages them in activities that increase their self-esteem. Being involved in extracurricular activities at school or church has proved to be of significant value in developing resiliency and strengths in response to a problematic life. Exposure to healthier ways of coping and relating and the opportunity to explore their individual talents is crucial for a child living in a troubled family. Every adult child can identify some one person who they believe made a positive difference in their life. That person did or said something that helped that child feel he or she was of value.

Tom's involvement in high school sports was his time out from home, giving him relief, but also sports offered him a source of esteem. Ellie still sees her junior high school boyfriend's parents. She considers them as having been surrogate parents who listened, validated her, and allowed her to just be a kid when she was with them in their home. Lew believes it was his uncle, whom he describes as a quiet man, who took time to allow Lew in his life. He allowed Lew to help with chores around the house, go on short vacations with his family, and showed up at Lew's school events. The message Lew got was that he was of value to this uncle, that he was worthy. What can seem so little to the giver can make a tremendous difference to the receiver.

Create and Maintain Positive Family Rituals

Healthy family rituals create a sense of belonging offering children a sense of pride. All families have rituals, but sadly for children raised with addition, healthy rituals are often decimated, and unhealthy rituals manifested. In addictive families, meal times are often times to be feared or don't exist. Bedtime is lonely. Rituals around holidays are ignored, dismissed, or are times of family scenes and trauma. Celebrations, be it birthdays, graduations or religious ceremonies, are times of great trepidation and unpredictability.

Building healthy rituals begins with identifying daily rituals (mealtimes, bedtime, after school time), and yearly rituals (birthdays and holidays) and then any other rituals that the family has created, (Saturday-runs to a yogurt store, service work on Sundays, etc.). What messages do these give the child? What can you do to reinforce a healthy ritual around the already existing ones, and what new ones can be incorporated? It is possible when children's parents don't live together that at least one parent can maintain healthy rituals. Sometimes, the rituals occur via extended family members. Whatever can be done to support this is most important.

Reshaping Roles

Reshaping roles is about attending to the emotional, mental, and behavioral deficits that result from the dysfunction within the family during a child's developmental years. These voids include not learning to relax, not knowing how to rely on others, not knowing how to follow or not knowing how to lead, never allowing one's own needs to be met, and the many other undeveloped coping mechanisms. Not only will these gaps create life-skill problems, but they may also predispose the children to marry addicts and/or engage in addictive disorders. The lack of healthy coping mechanisms often predisposes children to experience depression, anxiety, and relational problems.

When helping children understand addiction through talking about the real issues and teaching them to identify and express feelings while establishing healthy support networks, there is also a specific need to focus on reshaping roles.

The rigidity of the roles were adopted out of the severe need to bring consistency to a chaotic and unpredictable family system, to emotionally make sense of the moment. Children get to keep the strengths of their roles. The reshaping is to learn what was not safe. Children need an environment in which they can learn skills their natural survival techniques are not allowing them to learn. We want children to learn balance. The goal is not to take a responsible child and make him irresponsible or an adjusting child and make her inflexible or a placating child and make him totally egocentric. Nor do we want the mascot to lose his or her sense of humor. We want children to experience choice about how they respond to different situations.

The reshaping of roles generally means changing our expectations of children's behaviors and changing our behavior toward them. Instead of becoming immediately frustrated when the eight-year-old acts eight and insisting she behave like a little adult, allow her to display some of that normal eight-year-old behavior. This will require patience. When the placating child reaches out to placate one more time, rather than applaud, let him or her know you appreciate their thoughtfulness but you want to be alone and you are going to call an adult friend to talk. When the adjuster responds to open-ended questions with " I don't know," pause and reframe the questions where he has options to choose from. When the mascot uses her humor to distract, stay focused with what you expect from her in the moment.

Adults need to take responsibility where they can. Spreading the responsibility may mean providing a babysitter, even though the ten-year-old is extremely responsible and nearly as capable as the fifteen-year-old babysitter. It could mean that the parent gets up twenty minutes earlier in the morning and prepares a casserole. This makes the adult responsible for dinner and not the twelve-year-old. Children need your support and encouragement to make friends and to be involved in afterschool play activities. Applaud and encourage them to take time out to play and laugh.

Do not deemphasize the importance of responsibility with overly responsible children. Instead, emphasize parts of their characters they have not yet actualized—their spontaneity, playfulness, and ability to lean on someone and to recognize that they are not compelled to have all the answers. It is okay to make mistakes. Responsible children need to be praised and have their deeds acknowledged not only when they are doing their best and acting as strong leaders, but also when other endeavors take them out of the leadership role, such as playing on a team without being the captain. Remember, while these children demonstrate leadership qualities, this personality characteristic will be healthy only when it is not adopted as a matter of survival. Reinforce the children's natural need to share with and lean on others when they have to make decisions and work on projects. Let them know although they are bright and accomplished youngsters, they are still just that—youngsters.

Encourage children who are not overly responsible to take healthy risks and make decisions for themselves. They need to learn to trust their own decision-making processes. They need to find when they do make a decision that you will follow through and support them. Start with situations that are the least threatening and have the fewest possible negative consequences—what television show to watch, what to have for dinner, how to handle a project. These children must learn to feel good about themselves because of their own accomplishments and their own decisions, not because they seek approval. Remember, the placating child will gladly make a decision if that is what is necessary to obtain approval. The goal, however, is not to attain approval, it is to instill in children the ability to make their own healthy decisions, to learn organizational skills, and to know how to problem-solve. The mascot often takes risks but those risks are for the sake of attention, the risks that aid them would be in the area of taking responsibility for themselves.

It is normal that children will feel awkward about making changes. Change in any system, even when that change is positive, is often met with resistance. As you assist in reshaping roles, children may exhibit confusion, withdrawal, or anger. When the ten-year-old has been busy playing the mother and the little adult when you suggest she try to play hopscotch and giggle with her friends—behavior that has been totally out of her realm of reality—it's very likely she will initially push back or rebel in some way.

A similar rebellion will come from the adjusting child when you ask him to share his anger or hurt. For the son who managed to stare at the television while his father was ranting and raving and showed no signs of being affected, to share feelings now seems far beyond his present capabilities. The mascot is most likely to look at you as if you are speaking a foreign language.

To ask the placating child who has been taking care of everyone else's feelings to focus on herself rather than others is equally foreign. Being self-focused does not give her the satisfaction she felt in taking care of others. She has learned to feel good about herself only when she is helping others.

Reshaping roles needs to be done slowly and is more effective when several adults are involved in the process. Encourage extended family members, school personnel, family friends, and those who are in a child's life how they can be helpful.

Recommended reinforcing behaviors for responsible children:
- Give attention at times when the child is not achieving.
- Validate the child's intrinsic worth, and try to separate feelings of self-worth from achievements.
- Let the child know it's okay to make a mistake.
- Encourage the child to play.
- Emphasize parts of the child's character not yet actualized, i.e., playfulness, spontaneity, ability to rely on someone else.

Recommended reinforcing behaviors for adjusting children:

- Engage in one-to-one contact to learn more about the individual child.
- Point out and encourage the child's strengths, talents, and creativity.
- Bring them into decision-making process, giving them win-win choices.
- Engage in their personal interests.

Recommended reinforcing behaviors for placating children:
- Assist the child in focusing on him- or herself instead of others.
- Help this child play.
- When the child is assisting another, ask how he or she is feeling.
- Validate the child's intrinsic worth, separating his or her worth from his or her caretaking.
- Reinforce there are others who will take care of other people, that is not the child's job.

Recommended reinforcing behaviors for mascot:
- Give the child responsibilities with importance.
- Encourage responsible behavior.
- Hold the child accountable.
- Insist on eye contact.
- Encourage appropriate expression of humor.

For the acting-out child, recognize that this child is exhibiting unacceptable behavior because of family problems and the inability to get his or her needs met. Sometimes acting-out children were initially responsible and sensitive to others but found it brought them no satisfaction. The consequence of their dissatisfaction is rebellion— rebellion used to ward off pain. Many acting-out children have the ability to lead and can respond sensitively to others when in the right environment. These children must learn new productive outlets for anger; these children need validation and consistency in their lives.

Recommended reinforcing behaviors for acting-out children:
- Let the child know when behavior is inappropriate.

- Give the child compliments and encouragement whenever he or she takes responsibility for something.
- Develop empathy for the child by looking at what may lie underneath his or her attitude and behaviors.
- Set limits. Give clear explanations of the child's responsibilities and clear choices and consequences.
- Give the child opportunities for healthy leadership.

When reshaping roles be cautious though for children still in active addictive family. It may be unrealistic for them to let go of certain parts of their rigid roles within the home. A ten-year-old may be the adult within the home, but if we can help that ten-year-old be ten outside of the home, we are helping that child to develop more fully. For example, it may be more helpful for this child to do the laundry at home in order to have clean clothes for school, rather than to encourage her not to if it means no clean clothes. The flexibility of the adjuster may be exactly what is needed if she is still subject to personality changes of one or both parents. That said, you can still build in greater resiliency by offering the child additional coping skills.

People of all ages need help, advice, and guidance; these messages are best transmitted when both words and actions coincide.

Expectations in Parental Recovery

Katherine was twelve years old when her father was first getting sober. She had very little denial about her father's addiction and was thrilled her father had gone to a treatment program. Shortly after her father returned home, Katherine reported to her support group, "Everything is just really wonderful." She is smiling and has absolutely no problem in the world. Katherine believed because her father was now clean and sober he was going to wake up and no longer being anesthetized, which meant Dad was going to discover his twelve-year-old daughter. But Katherine's father had been an addict all of her life and that meant he was going to discover how little he knew his young daughter. Katherine's life just couldn't remain all roses. In a matter of weeks, her mother said that she was having a difficult time in school. One day, I challenged her, "Katherine, things aren't fine, are they?"

"Oh yeah, they are just fine," she responded.

I said, "No, things are not just fine. Things are often not good even though a parent gets sober."

In the form of an art exercise, she drew a picture of her dad looking happy, but she looked sad. Underneath the picture of their faces, she wrote, "I have a hard time understanding why my dad goes to those meetings every night, and why he is not home."

Katherine had a lot of expectations, many of which were fantasies, about how she and her father were going to spend so much time together now that her dad was sober. The fact was, in his initial recovery, her dad was so actively involved in twelve-step meetings that he spent nearly as little time home as when he was using. Katherine did not understand; she was confused and very angry, and she immediately reverted to her denial system in order to protect herself from the feelings she was experiencing. Her father did need all those meetings. It is not sufficient for a counselor to explain this need to children and partners. Katherine needed her father to share his feelings about the meetings and to share his thoughts about recovery. If parents need time away from families to attend meetings, it is important for them to explain and share with the family how vital and necessary this part of their recovery program is for them. Nonetheless, Katherine's father still needs to find ways to connect to his daughter. With healthy communication and even a small amount of concentrated father-daughter time around something that Katherine was interested in, be it her bird collection, her art, or a video game, Katherine could have the patience needed to not build up resentments.

Sydney encountered a similar situation with her children. She found that by telling her kids what she learned at each meeting, making a point to always eat dinner with them and to always say good night, and by designating special time every two weeks with each of her children, she didn't need to reduce the number of meetings she attended nor feel guilty about her parenting.

People struggle with parenting when they have not had healthy parental modeling, when their emotional growth has been stunted due to their addiction and or codependency. While recovery doesn't suddenly give someone parenting skills, it does give them a foundation for honesty and accountability. Due to guilt there is this pull to give a child whatever they want or to simply stay away from parenting. Essential though is remembering a parent's job is to be a child's best parent not their best friend. There are many resources to guide parents, but it all begins with commitment to your own recovery.

We cannot always change the environment children are raised in, but we can change what they believe about themselves.

We need to help children overcome the need to medicate or run from their feelings. We need to assist them in developing problem-solving skills. We need to help them know they are of value and they are worthy. It sounds like a lot, but if we are willing to offer education about addiction, validate children in their feelings, assist them with problem-solving, respond to protection issues, and facilitate a greater support system, we will genuinely create more resilient children who have far greater choice about how they will live their lives.

CHAPTER NINE

Healing Resources

No one heals in isolation. Addiction and its impact on others is a disease of disconnection. Disconnection from others and disconnection from self. To heal, people need others to begin and sustain that process. Recovery is about connection, connection to self and others.

"Yes, but . . . yes, but . . . it wasn't that bad. Yes, but . . . no one would really understand. Yes, but . . . I have been out of the home for years now. Yes, but . . . I do really love my parent(s). Yes, but . . . Others have it worse." Those are often the spoken words or the inner dialogue that occurs when the adult child starts to think about reaching out for help.

There is always someone who has suffered more loss, experienced more trauma than you. But that does not negate *your* pain, your loss, your trauma. There are people who understand and it doesn't matter how old you are. You are not betraying your mother, your father, or your family by owning your truth. If there is an act of betrayal, it is with the disease, the addictive disorder. If there is an act of betrayal, it is with yourself if you do not allow yourself to heal. You deserve to heal from the pain of the past. You deserve to no longer live a script but to live with choices.

"I do want recovery, but I want it to be pain-free, thank you." "I want recovery, but I prefer to do it by myself." These are two examples of resistance that adult children often present as they think about contemplating addressing their family of origin issues. These two resistances speak to the fear of feelings and using self-reliance as a defense. For many years, staying away from feelings has worked, for a while. No longer. Self-reliance is a nice attribute but rigid self-reliance is based on not being willing to trust others.

For a moment, imagine the depth of your pain and grief as a strong forceful wind. If you were to stand in the face of the wind, feet and legs held tightly together, back rigidly straight, and arms down by your side, it would easily blow you over. You are probably smart enough to realize that and run for shelter. Most of us run for shelter through work, relationships, drugs or alcohol, sex, or use of money. But if you were to lean forward with feet slightly apart, knees bent, arms slightly away from your body, you may find yourself swaying in the face of that strong wind, but you don't have to run or be blown away. You now have the potential of finding your strength as you remain standing.

In addition to balance and flexibility, it is even more likely you will be able to remain standing with the support and help of others. To live in an addictive family is to live a life of isolation. You have known isolation for too long. You deserve to allow others to be a part of your process. They will also shine the light and provide the hope when that is difficult to do for yourself.

Reaching out and making that first contact with a helping resource is a big step. The act of searching the internet for a name, sending that inquiry via email, picking up the phone, dialing the number, and asking to speak to someone who can help only takes seconds. The process that leads to reaching out for help—the debates with yourself, telling yourself you can handle the problems alone, the never-ending, continuous cycle of fear, anger, loneliness, guilt—all have taken their psychological and physical toll on you and your family. Allowing others to be a part of your process and seeking support is a sign of strength not weakness. It is a sign of self-respect and worth, believing you are deserving.

Resources

Twelve-step groups are the most common type of mutual support groups for people who want to recover from any addiction and its familial impact. In the Appendix, a list of twelve-step fellowships is provided along with contact information. Self-help groups involve no professional counselors and do not document one's involvement. They are free of charge to all who wish to participate. They are groups made up of people who identify with a common problem and are looking for a common solution, a way of helping themselves and each other. Participating in a group process with others who identify with similar issues helps you learn to value yourself, to overcome fears, to begin to trust in self as well as others.

These fellowships have demonstrated themselves to be extremely helpful resources for millions of people worldwide. They provide opportunity for children, partners/spouses, or the addicted person to better understand the addiction and how it is affecting their lives. They offer every member a program of recovery, allowing each individual an avenue for feeling better about him- or herself and helping him or her continue to live more a productive life. Self-help groups offer people an opportunity to realize their experiences and feelings are not unique but, in fact, very similar to problems that each member of the group has experienced.

The validation that occurs within a group setting reduces shame. The dysfunctional family rules of Don't Talk, Don't Trust, and Don't Feel are broken. When the principles of the programs are practiced people learn compassion for self, personal accountability, self-forgiveness, self-respect, and honesty. In this process you find your way to honoring yourself.

An important unifying aspect of these groups is that they practice a rule of anonymity. This means your name, your job, or your status in the community are not relevant. The unemployed are as important as the employed, the less educated are as important as the more educated. Last names are not used. Everyone is considered equal with fellow beings who suffer the same as you.

Al-Anon and Nar-Anon are twelve-step groups for family members. While partners, spouses, and parents tend to be the family members most in attendance, both groups are open to all family members. Many adult children have embraced Al-Anon, a program that began in the 1950s, and find strength in its longevity. It has created literature specifically for the adult child.

Adult children have also embraced the programs of ACA (Adult Children of Alcoholics /Dysfunctional families). ACA began in the latter

1980s and has experienced a resurgence today. Its Big Book, first published in 2006, often thought of as the Red Book, has given the program both breadth and depth.

Codependency Anonymous has remained another popular twelve-step group for adult children and partners with its focus on relationships.

There are twelve-step meetings for nearly all addictive disorders, and many are listed in the Appendix.

Not everyone feels comfortable in a twelve-step meeting. And there are other options of self-help particularly for the addicted person. Rational Recovery, SMART, Women for Sobriety, are the most well-known non-twelve-step programs and most available in the urban areas.

Also many recovery groups offer options for online meetings. With the pandemic of 2020, utilizing online resources has proven invaluable and is likely to become more integrated into people's recovery practices.

I'm glad my dad doesn't drink any more because he talks with me, & I understand him better, I also like the people at A. A. because they don't just walk away from the kids, we go on a lot of picnics with A. A. and they are more fun than being with a bunch of drunk adults!!

Some adult children find they need the support and structure of treatment programs for their addiction and/or mental health issues, most specifically depression, self-harm, or anxiety. When issues are less acute, it may be possible to find a workshop format that helps you. Workshops usually range from three days to two-week stays. These are usually recommended when you want more structure and more concentrated time than what outpatient psychotherapy may offer.

Adult children strongly benefit from psychotherapy. My bias is we can all benefit from therapy, but I would strongly suggest it if you:

- Are experiencing signs of depression and anxiety.
- Are engaged in a pattern of self-destructive behaviors that can range from victimization in relationships, repetitive painful relationships, and self-harm.
- Have attempted to make constructive changes in your life and have been unable to do so.
- Have a history of physical or sexual abuse.

In seeking psychotherapy I recommend working with a trauma-informed therapist who understands addiction in the family, is familiar with the concepts of being an adult child, and understands codependency.

If you are engaged in behaviors such as spending, gambling, gaming, porn and other sexual acts, etc., that are interfering with major aspects of your life or you are using drugs and alcohol and having difficulty stopping when it is interfering in major aspects of your life—it is best you seek an addiction program or a therapist who specializes in addiction to make an appropriate assessment and can offer direction for level of care. That may be to continue with a specific therapist, it could be an intensive outpatient program, or it could also be an inpatient treatment program.

It is important to honor your coping mechanisms, they were critical to your survivorship. Recovery doesn't involve being critical of what you needed to do to protect yourself while you were growing up.

Addicted people do achieve abstinence and find recovery; family members do get well, but first, you need to ask for help.

my mom Feels better and I'm
Feeling the Same way

Jack, age 12

Resources for Children

People outside of the immediate family have a normal, and perhaps justifiable, fear of meddling in others' family affairs. Problems between parents and children regarding dress codes, money, or behavior are usually resolved within the confines of the family unit. An outsider who takes sides invariably gets the brunt of ill feelings after family members have reconciled these minor differences. But addiction is not a minor problem. Becoming an ally to the child is perhaps the first step toward the possibility of his or her healing. You may not change the home situation, but you can be a vital source in helping children withstand the pressures of the confusion in their family. Play the role of the listener—listen, console, and help validate the child's feelings. Offer guidance as it seems appropriate. But remember, the best guidance can be given by a qualified helping professional.

Children come into contact with people who play a variety of roles in their lives—parents, extended family members, friends, neighbors, teachers, counselors, doctors, judges—and each person is in a position to offer different kinds of help and support. The more people make themselves available as knowledgeable, skilled resources, the wider the spectrum and the greater the opportunities for help available to children, whether young, adolescent, or adult.

It is my hope that people not underestimate the amount of difference they can make in the life of a child, no matter how hopeless the situation may appear. A bond with a caring person is one of the most significant factors as to why some children from addictive families develop strengths and others do not. This is typically someone who allows that child to be age-appropriate, to not have to be the adult. This is someone who believes the child and will listen. Someone who says in words or behavior, "I care," and "You are important to me." This type of relationship allows that child to internalize worth and, as a consequence, reject the shaming behaviors and messages that may also be coming from a troubled family life.

Vanessa, who is now thirty-three, felt strongly about locating a counselor who had worked with her when she was only fifteen. At that time, Vanessa's parents were living on the streets and she had been put into a group home for approximately three months. She now wanted to say thank you. When the counselor asked what she remembered specifically about the counseling, she replied, "I have no idea what you did, but I know that you loved me."

Sometimes it is not what we do; it is what we feel and then have the ability to convey. Genuinely believing she was loved was the intangible gift this young woman hung on to and from which she found strength. That was more than she had ever experienced. And then she pulled out a journal and said, "You did ask me to keep a journal and to this day I do that." The journaling was a daily source of release and possibly strength but having felt loved was most important.

It is my contention children growing up with addiction suffer unhealthy consequences due to lack of involvement with other people, not from concerned involvement.

Taking Responsibility

Children affected by addiction will be adequately addressed and helped only when we, lay people and professionals alike, begin to take responsibility. Everyone who has access to these children needs to take some responsibility. The possibilities are many and vary, from:

- Talk with a family member.

- Ask the board you sit on to address the issue.
- Ask a clergyperson to address this issue with peers.
- Ask a physician to identify the impact addiction has on a family when it is recognized.
- Develop specific treatment curriculum and programs for children of addiction.
- Discuss addiction when identified.
- Suggest and refer to resources when indicated.

These actions take a willingness to become involved. Do not underestimate the impact you have, no matter how limited in power or time. Few helping resources have all of the ideal means, staff, space, money, or time necessary to develop the comprehensive services desired. But if every one assesses what can be done with the means at hand, they can actualize resources on the spot. With even a little greater effort, intermediate and long-range goals can be developed. To say, "We just can't do it all" is irresponsible behavior on our part, which is really saying, "We don't care enough."

Everyone who has access to a child needs to take responsibility. If you are willing to ask yourself what help you can provide, then you are taking the first step.

Together we can break the Don't Talk rule and break the generational cycle of addiction.

I FEEL LIKE I'VE BEEN ON A ROLLACOASTER FOR A REAL LONG TIME. I WANT OFF.

JANICE, 44

Appendix

When I initially wrote *It Will Never Happen to Me* it was based on my clinical work. At times, I was challenged for being anecdotal, writing only from the experience of my clinical practice and not science-based research. I knew research was needed, and I also knew it took several years to complete. I trusted my intuition, and I was not willing to let another generation of people go unidentified, unacknowledged, misunderstood, and to go without resources. I believed with all my heart that the research would follow and support what I and others were discovering about the impact of growing up in a family impacted by addiction. Due to the energy behind the adult-child movement, researchers became interested and today research data is readily accessible.

Adverse Childhood Experiences Study
I want to single out what is one of the largest studies ever conducted on the relationship between maltreatment in childhood and long-term effects on health and well-being, the Adverse Childhood Experiences Study, known as ACES. This study began in the 1990s at Kaiser Permanente San Diego by Robert Anda, MD, and Vincent Felliti, MD, and continues today through the Center of Disease Control and Prevention. The primary investigators looked at the following adverse experiences:

- Physical abuse.
- Verbal abuse.
- Sexual abuse.
- Physical neglect.

- Emotional neglect.
- Witnessing of domestic violence.
- Alcohol or other substance abusers in the home.
- Mentally ill or suicidal household members.
- Parental marital discord evidenced by separation or divorce.
- Having a household member serve time in prison.

Sadly, all of those are reflected repeatedly in the stories throughout this book.

Findings would show that:

- Childhood trauma was very common, regardless of socioeconomic class and education.
- There was a direct link between childhood trauma and adult onset of chronic health diseases that includes heart disease, lung cancer, diabetes, and many autoimmune diseases.
- There was a dramatic link between childhood trauma and social and emotional issues, mental health issues and addiction, as well as suicide, being violent, and being a victim of violence.
- Additional types of trauma increased the risk of health, social, and emotional problems and addiction.
- People usually experience more than one type of trauma.

People who experience the accumulative effects of growing up with a cluster of adverse childhood experiences tend to be those who fill our family service agencies, therapy offices, addiction programs, and mental and primary healthcare systems because childhood stress was more than the body/brain could handle. A child's brain is simply not equipped to digest or fully process ongoing relationship trauma.

For more information on ACE studies, search the internet under Adverse Childhood Experiences Study.

National Association for Children of Addiction

National Association for Children of Addiction (NACOA) has been providing information and education to help COAs of all ages since

1983. NACOA is a policy development center and a central point of input for children's health, welfare advocates, and service providers. Over the years it has provided significant materials to school systems, interfaith communities, and medical schools and practitioners. It is the national voice for children of addiction. (ww.nacoa.org)

Camp Mariposa: Part of the Eluna Network

Camp Mariposa is a national addiction prevention and mentoring program for youth who have been impacted by substance abuse in their families. It is offered free of charge to all families.

Children ages nine through twelve attend weekend camps multiple times a year. Campers participate in fun traditional camp activities combined with education and support exercises led by mental health professionals and trained mentors. Additional educational, social, and mentoring activities are offered for campers, teens, and their families throughout the year. It strongly serves our highly marginalized children who sadly know the experience of addiction and trauma in the family. If a young person is fortunate to live in a locale that offers Camp Mariposa, it is an invaluable resource. (https://elunanetwork.org/camps-programs/camp-mariposa/)

Self-Help Fellowships

www.adultchildren.org Adult Children of Alcoholics/Dysfunctional
Families 562.595.7831

www.al-anon.org Al-Anon (for friends and family of people with
alcoholism) 757.563.1600

www.al-anon.alateen.org Alateen (a fellowship of young Al-Anon
members, usually teenagers affected by someone's drinking) 757.563.1600

www.asca12step.org Adult Survivors of Child Abuse Anonymous
(recovery program for all survivors of childhood abuse and trauma)

www.chapter9-nyc.org Chapter 9—Couples in Recovery Anonymous
(a program of couples working together) 212.946.1874

www.co-anon.org Co-Anon and Co-Ateen (for relatives and friends
of cocaine addicts) 520.513.5028

www.coda.org Co-Dependents Anonymous (CoDA) 602.277.7991 or
888.444.2359 (toll-free English) 888.444.2379 (toll-free Spanish)

www.cosa-recovery.org COSA (for co-addicts whose lives have been
affected by other people's compulsive sexual behavior) 866.899.2672

www.familiesanonymous.org Families Anonymous (for anyone in recovery from the effects of a loved one's addiction) 847.294.5877

www.gam-anon.org Gam-Anon (for anyone affected by the gambling problem of a family member, loved one, or friend) 718.352.1671

www.naasca.org National Association of Adult Survivors of Child Abuse (child abuse trauma prevention, intervention, and recovery)

www.nar-anon.org Nar-Anon (for relatives and friends of people with drug addiction) 310.534.8188

www.recovering-couples.org Recovering Couples Anonymous 781.794.1456

www.sanon.org S-Anon and S-Ateen (for people who have been affected by other's sexual behavior) 615.833.3152

www.12step.org offers information, tools, and resources for organizing a twelve-step program

Substance Addiction

www.aa.org Alcoholics Anonymous 212.870.3400

www.alladdictsanonymous.org All Addicts Anonymous (for anyone dealing with any addiction) 888.422.2476

http://cdaweb.org Chemically Dependent Anonymous (for anyone seeking freedom from drug or alcohol addiction) 888.232.4673

www.ca.org Cocaine Anonymous 310.559.5833

www.crystalmeth.org Crystal Meth Anonymous 213.488.4455

www.lifering.org LifeRing Secular Recovery (network of individuals seeking to live in recovery) 800.811.4142

www.marijuana-anonymous.org Marijuana Anonymous 800.766.6779

www.na.org Narcotics Anonymous 818.773.9999

www.pillsanonymous.org Pills Anonymous

www.nicotine-anonymous.org 877.879.6422

www.smartrecovery.org SMART Recovery (helps people recover from all types of addiction and addictive behaviors) 866.951.5357

www.sossobriety.org Secular Organizations for Sobriety (helps individuals achieve and maintain sobriety/abstinence from alcohol and drug addiction, food addiction, and more) 323.666.4295

www.womenforsobriety.org Women for Sobriety (helping women overcome alcohol and other addictions) 215.536.8026

Process Addiction

www.cgaa.info Computer Gaming Addicts Anonymous

www.debtorsanonymous.org Debtors Anonymous 718.453.2743

www.gamblersanonymous.org Gamblers Anonymous 888.424.3577

www.netaddictionrecovery.com Internet and Tech Addiction Anonymous 818.773.9999

www.olganon.org Online Gamers Anonymous 612.245.1115

www.sexaa.org Sex Addicts Anonymous 713.869.4902

www.slaafws.org Sex and Love Addicts Anonymous 210.828.7922

www.sa.org Sexaholics Anonymous 615.370.6062

www.sca-recovery.org Sexual Compulsives Anonymous 212.606.3778

www.sexualrecovery.org Sexual Recovery Anonymous 646.450.8565

Food Addiction
http://aba12steps.org Anorexics and Bulimics Anonymous
780.318.6355

www.ceahow.org Compulsive Eaters Anonymous (HOW)
562.342.9344

www.foodaddictsanonymous.org Food Addicts Anonymous
772.878.9657

www.foodaddicts.org Food Addicts in Recovery Anonymous
781.932.6300

www.oa.org Overeaters Anonymous 505.891.2664

Other Fellowships
www.draonline.org Dual Recovery Anonymous (for people with
addiction and mental illness) 913.991.2703

www.emotionsanonymous.org Emotions Anonymous (for people
working toward recovery from emotional difficulties) 651.647.9712

Christian Twelve-Step Fellowships

For a more complete list of Christian twelve-step programs, organizations, groups, and ministries, visit the website of the National Association of Christian Recovery **www.nacr.org**.

www.alcoholicsforchrist.com Alcoholics for Christ (for adults who have grown up in an alcoholic family system or any other dysfunctional system) 248.399.9955

www.alcoholicsvictorious.org Alcoholics Victorious (for people recovering from the effects of alcoholism or drug addiction)

www.overcomersoutreach.org Overcomers Outreach (for individuals, their families, and loved ones who suffer from the consequences of any addictive behavior) 562.698.9000

Please do not assume the word *anonymous* automatically identifies an organization or website as a twelve-step fellowship. Some enthusiast sites and retailers use the word in their names. For example, Gamers Anonymous is a video game store, and screenaddicts.co.uk is a website for film, television, and video game enthusiasts. However, Computer Gaming Addicts Anonymous (cgaa.info), On-Line Gamers Anonymous (olganon. org), Computer Addicts Anonymous (computeraa.wordpress.com), and Internet and Tech Addiction Anonymous (netaddictionrecovery.com) are all legitimate twelve-step fellowships.

Professional Assistance

www.emdria.org Eye Movement Desensitization and Reprocessing (EMDR)

www.iitap.com International Institute for Trauma and Addiction Professionals (sex addiction and trauma) (IITAP)

www.nbcc.org National Board of Certified Counselors

therapists.psychologytoday.com is a directory of therapists, counselors, support groups, and treatment centers in the United States

findtreatment.samhsa.gov/locator/stateagencies links to state mental health agencies' lists of mental health and/or addiction programs and professionals within each state

naadac.org/sap-directory Nationwide directory of substance abuse professionals in the United States

verywell.com/canadian-treatment-centres-63615 Nationwide directory of Canadian alcohol and drug treatment and rehab centers

Also by Claudia Black, PhD

Claudia Black is the author of over fifteen books, all available via Central Recovery Press. See the Claudia Black Library at CentralRecoveryPress.com for a full list and descriptions of her books, CDs, and videos. Those that accompany *It Will Never Happen to Me* in expanding thought and recovery include:

Unspoken Legacy: Addressing the Impact of Trauma and Addiction within the Family

Straight Talk from Claudia Black: What Recovering Parents Should Tell Their Kids about Drugs and Alcohol

Repeat After Me: A Workbook for Adult Children Overcoming Dysfunctional Family Systems

Changing Course: Healing from Loss, Abandonment, and Fear

My Dad Loves Me, My Dad Has a Disease (a book for children ages five through twelve)

CDs

A Time for Healing from Abandonment and Shame

Imageries

Letting Go

Putting the Past Behind

Acknowledgments

Many people have helped to make this book a reality. Over the years, I have received support from a multitude of professional and personal friends. Yet the greatest motivator has continued to be the many young and adult children who shared parts of their lives with me. Their courage, vulnerability, and honesty inspired me on all levels. It is those lives that give the emotional depth and incredibly rich meaning to *It Will Never Happen to Me*. This book has been written in honor of each and every one who has traveled on this healing journey.

While I have had strong support from so many, there is a group of people who have been more directly involved in the creating of *It Will Never Happen to Me*. A special thank you to Renee Cavalier, Joan Fiset, and Jane Middleton Moz for their poetry, and Peter Nardi for his story. Your words, written many years ago, have offered validation and hope for the journey.

Victoria Danzig, Martha Ranson, Margaret Hillman, Lynn Sanford, Jael Greenleaf, Deborah Smith Parker, and Muriel Zink played a direct role in the first edition, giving their support and feedback to me and continue to be a part of my life.

Bob Stein, Annie Doce, Barry Levy, and Anne Marie Piontek—you will not be forgotten for your original contributions.

Margaret Cork, author of *Forgotten Children*, and renowned family therapist Virginia Satire, my professional inspirations to give voice to children of addiction. Thank you.

It Will Never Happen to Me is truly my child, a very special child. I can offer it only because of the important people in my life. While many of them have already been acknowledged, I need to add to this list my grandmother Margaret Dolquist, a lifelong mentor, who passed away at the age of ninety-seven. My long-standing friends Shelia Fields and Lorie Dwinell, your unconditional support of me has always been most valued. I am grateful for the friendships of Bob Martin, Mary Carol Melton, and Sis Wenger. I have been blessed with their validation and enthusiasm for my writings and work. A special thanks as well to my friends Ginny Brown and Russel Zink—angels who are always there to remind me to take care of me.

Sadly, my father and my childhood friend, Debbie, have died from their addictions. I would like to acknowledge the incredible meaning and gifts they gave me in their life.

Tammy Stark worked for me for over thirteen years. Her life passion was in her dedication to the readers of my many books. She believed wholeheartedly in the recovery journey that would lie ahead. While invisible to most by name, may she be remembered for her commitment to the many readers.

Sandi Klein, my assistant, you have been invaluable help in this edition and with over two decades of being my right-hand person for whom I am forever grateful.

While I have been quite visible to the world, my mother and sister, Jana have been my champions. My work would lead me to share about my personal life that would reflect upon theirs; they have stood with me in pride and love. Thank you. Let me thank my stepfather, Tom, as well. You were a light in our lives.

There is no other person I am more indebted for the fact this book exists than my late husband, Jack Fahey. He was there for the gnashing of teeth that came with the many rewrites, the emotional pain that was tapped attempting to speak to the vulnerability of living with addiction, and the joy in witnessing the journey into recovery.

Thank you all.

About the Author

Claudia Black is a renowned author and trainer internationally recognized for her pioneering and contemporary work with family systems and addictive disorders. She is a Senior Fellow and the Clinical Architect at the Claudia Black Young Adult Center at The Meadows Treatment Center in Arizona. As a result, she continues to have hands-on therapy experiences with young people often raised with addiction. She is the author of numerous books, including *Unspoken Legacy*, *Straight Talk*, and *Repeat After Me*.

Printed in the USA
CPSIA information can be obtained
at www.ICGtesting.com
JSHW020825110624
64551JS00006B/382